Visual
Management
The Lean Way

Visual Management

The Lean Way

Rajiv Tiwari

White Falcon
Publishing

www.whitefalconpublishing.com

Visual Management - The Lean Way
Rajiv Tiwari

www.whitefalconpublishing.com

ISBN - 978-93-87193-93-2

DEDICATION

Dedicated to my parents and wife, their love and support always encourages me to come out of my comfort zone.

I would also like to dedicate this book to my organization, HCL Technologies for providing an environment of creative thinking and lots of learning.

We are not called as employees rather Ideapreneurs and that reflects a lot about the organization's culture.

ABOUT THE AUTHOR

RAJIV TIWARI

11 years of experience in Business excellence, with Analytical and Consulting experience across multiple domains like Telecom, F&A, Healthcare and IT Infra.

He did his Graduation in Electrical Engineering from West Bengal University of Technology, and got campus recruitment to Tech Mahindra. This entry to ITES organization gave him the opportunity to work with the Business Excellence group.

He has worked with Steria India Ltd, now Sopra Steria, and is currently working with HCL.

In a short span of time, he started working as a Business consultant, approbation goes to his multiple domain exposure and continuous appetite for learning.

During his professional career, he completed his PGDBA (Marketing) from SCDL.

HE IS ALSO CERTIFIED IN:

Six Sigma Black Belt
Lean Competency Certification – Level (1a, 1b and 1c) from Cardiff University
ITIL V3 Intermediate
PMP

The industry exposure and learnings have helped him to build a strong knowledge base.

He is a strong believer of Lean Methodology, and has immense interest in it. As quoted by him, *"To implement Lean one needs to be passionate, full of positive thought process, a strong team player and have hunger for improvement."*

This book reflects his interest in the subject, as Visual Management is one of the critical aspects of Lean.

Rajiv currently stays in Noida (Delhi/NCR) with his family. He loves reading books related to IT, business and politics. His favorite fun time is watching cartoon movies with his son.

His aim is to spread awareness about effective and efficient deployment of Lean in organizations, so that people take this as a mindset change rather than just another tool of improvement. The more aware the leaders and the bottom layer will be, long-lasting will be the benefits.

REVIEWER AND GUIDE

PRADEEP SINGH SINGROHA

17+ years of experience in: – Program Management – Analytics – Lean-IT - Operations & SLA Management – Process Improvement

Consulting experience in domains like Utilities, Finance, Pharmaceutical, Media & Entertainment

A keen planner, strategist & implementer having gained comprehensive experience in numerous process improvement projects & business excellence initiatives with respect to cost, resource deployment, time over-runs and quality compliance.

Proven record of excellent performance in delivering breakthrough business results, leading business excellence initiatives including Six Sigma and change realization

Experience of working in United States, Europe, Asia Pacific and Middle East for fortune customers

Delivered 600+ Hrs. of trainings on Green Belt, Yellow Belt, White Belt, Lean, Statistical Process Control and Basic Statistics

HE IS ALSO CERTIFIED IN:

Six Sigma Master Black Belt from Indian Statistical Institute

Auditor for ISO-14001 (Environment Management System), ISO-9001 & ISO-20000

Lean-IT Certified

ITIL V3 Foundation Certified

Pradeep believes that *"Lean can transform the business and can bring a cultural shift to the organization from reactive to proactive, transferring the onus to accountable individuals, traditional thinking to creative thinking. It can do wonders for business fraternity, important is keen interest and involvement of top leadership. Lean inputs are critical for business transformation through Automation and Artificial Intelligence"*

This book is a brainchild of Pradeep, he has performed critical review on topics covered. His thought was to avoid jargons and being too technical and share the experiences with readers.

OUR INSPIRATIONAL SOURCE

NAVIN SABHARWAL

Navin is an Innovator, Thought Leader, Author and Consultant in areas of AI and Machine Learning, Cloud Computing, Big Data Analytics, Software Product Development, Engineering and R&D.

Responsible for IP Development & Service Delivery in the Areas of AI and Machine Learning, Automation products, Cloud Computing, Public Cloud AWS, Microsoft Azure, VMWare Private Cloud, Microsoft Private Cloud, Data Center Automation, Analytics for IT Operations, IT Service Management.

Author of:

- First Steps Cloud Computing (Createspace)
- Apache CloudStack Cloud Computing (Packt Publishing)
- Cloud Capacity Planning (Apress)
- Automation using Opscode Chef, A Devops Approach (Apress)
- Big Data, NOSQL Architecting MongoDB (CreateSpace)
- Big Data, MongoDB (Apress)
- Hands on Docker (Apress)

Navin likes to build self-sustaining teams who can take up the products and solutions to greater heights. He has successfully created high performance teams for niche products and solutions.

He has set-up and managed large delivery teams for Service Integration in the areas of:

- Public Cloud Computing (Microsoft Azure, Amazon Web Services)
- Private Cloud Computing (Microsoft, VMware)
- Cloud Computing (HP Stack, BMC CLM, CA Cloud Automation Suite)
- IT Infrastructure & Application Monitoring (SCOM, Nagios, Zenos etc.)
- IT Service Management Products (HPSM, HPSD)
- Service Automation (BMC Bladelogic, BMC Atrium orchestrator, CA Server Automation, ITPAM, HP Opsware, HP Operations Orchestrator, Opalis)
- CSI and Reporting and Analytics (Business Objects, Cognos, Dashboards)

ACKNOWLEDGMENTS

While working on this book I realized that it's easy to prepare slide decks and presentations, compared to penning down your learning and thoughts in a book.

I could not have achieved this without the support and guidance of my Manager and Mentor, Pradeep Singh Singroha, who was a reviewer and guide for me throughout.

I am also glad to have colleagues, who helped me in completing this work, and I would really like to thank:

- Shailesh Chakraborty – for providing me excellent examples which are a part of this book
- Gaurav Ghosh – who helped me in finalizing images which I am sure readers will like
- Surajit Bhattacharjee – my friend and guide since my college days
- Trilochana Bhardwaj – for being consistently after me to push my limits to complete the book as soon as I could.

I am really grateful to my entire Lean team, rather than a team I will call it a Knowledge Bank, where exchange of experiences happens every day.

CONTENTS

INTRODUCTION

Visuals are an integral part of our surroundings, be it home, office, transportation, healthcare, shopping malls, restaurants or politics.

Now someone may ask from where did politics come into the picture? Can you think of any political parties without a symbol? Have you ever thought why they need a symbol, even though they have a name?

Similarly, think of any organization, they are very specific about their logo, brand symbol and color coding. All these factors hold a significance, it talks a lot about the organization's vision and mission. The same holds true for any political outfits or social groups we see around us.

Think about any blockbuster movie, what if you get a 200-page script of the movie and someone asks you to read the same rather than watching it on screen? I am sure majority of us will choose latter, even though we get the script free to read.

That's the power of visualizing something.

Visualization is only said to be effective when it creates an appeal among the targeted audience.

What if suddenly someone asks us to watch movies on a black & white screen? I am sure we can try for once just to get a feel of it but it will not be a preferable way. Colors enhance the appeal and provide better visualization.

The plots which filmmakers set as background, the colors, the environment all make a combined effect on our mind, followed by a strong story line and performance of the artists.

To transform a script on paper into a blockbuster movie, required is a correct mix of all the above characteristics.

Let's discuss some more scenarios of our daily life. We daily see the road signals. Assume that instead of three different colors Red, Green and Amber, if it was a single color Yellow for all the three sections with numbers flashing on them

1 = STOP
2 = Go
3 = Watch & Go
Don't you think it will confuse you?

The thought is that visuals work well in sync with the colors we use, with an understanding of how human brain will interpret the same.

Red always symbolizes danger, hence either in traffic signals, railway signals, Red is used to signal that we have to stop, else we will be in trouble.

Think of our office scenarios—you may be in manufacturing, IT, healthcare, telecom, etc. You will be able to relate that if deadlines are missed, the status turns to Red, which symbolizes urgency, something is not right and immediate action is required.

While reading through the pages did you notice the number of times Red is written? That's what the impact of colors is.

If I put Green everywhere in the project or production status, it's a natural feeling that people will interpret as everything is perfect.

Visuals play an important role in our life. The idea behind writing this book is to make the readers understand and implement an effective visual management environment at workplace, based on lean principles and best practices followed across organizations.

Effective visual management triggers action, drives right behavior, provides better engagement platform within the team and leads to enhance productivity and quality.

Many teams or organizations claim that they practice visual management, but based on my observations visual management is not just about putting pictures and graphs around the floor. If they are not discussed and noticed by the people working there or if it does not trigger any action then it's just a wallpaper.

CHAPTER 1

KEY NOTES

- Visuals are an integral part of our surroundings.
- Visuals create a bigger impact compared to normal text.
- Visuals do not mean painting office walls with charts, smart arts and putting all possible metrics.

QUIZ

1. **Visual Management is:**
   a. Nicely Painted Walls
   b. Walls with Organization's Objectives
   c. Visual Boards (Electronic or Manual) with metrics and stuff to trigger action proactively if anything moves from its standard state
   d. A notice board

2. **Visual Management is not applicable in:**
   a. Manufacturing Industry
   b. Automobile Industry
   c. Healthcare
   d. None of the above

3. **Visual Management is all about**
   a. Bar charts and Pie charts on boards
   b. Putting team structure on boards
   c. Highlighting the major escalations
   d. It's a combination of Team Objective, Metrics, Issues and Key success items

4. **Benefits of Visual Management**
   a. Team Cohesiveness
   b. Improves individual ownership and accountability
   c. Focused and proactive approach
   d. All of the above

5. **Visual boards must be prepared with only black and blue color**
   a. True
   b. False

ABOUT VISUAL MANAGEMENT

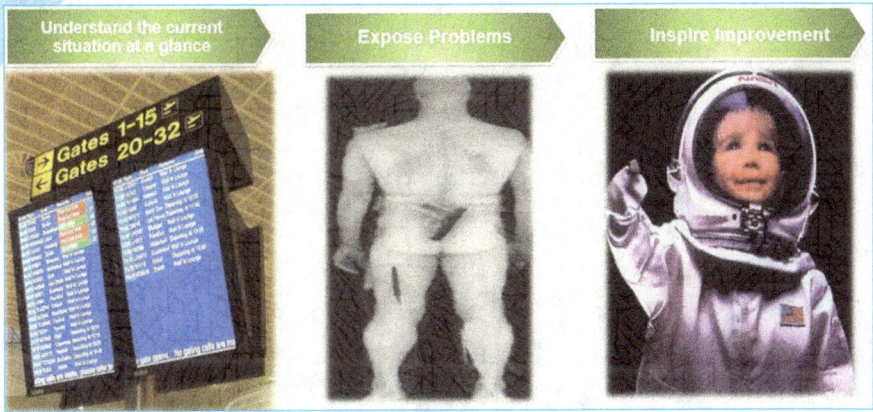

To enable everyone to immediately see deviations from the optimum state of work and working, and to enable immediate corrective action:

- Create an environment which highlights deviations
- Develop the workforce that knows the right thing to do when they encounter deviation
- Empower the workforce to do the right thing
- Using visual aids to manage the operation/project, including schedules, performance tracking, and project status
- Display Targeted versus Actual

- It's a way of communicating to a broad audience, in a clear manner and it quickly puts information in the hands of those who can take action.
- Make information physical, get it out of the computer
- Progress – Work tracking/Status
- Bottlenecks
- Actual Vs. Estimated/Target Key Performance Indicators
- Problems – What needs attention?
- Results – How did we do?
- Anyone should be able to go into a work area and know what's going on within a few minutes without asking many questions.

WHERE VISUAL MANAGEMENT WORKS?

Significance of visuals, rather than just naming an image impacts more.

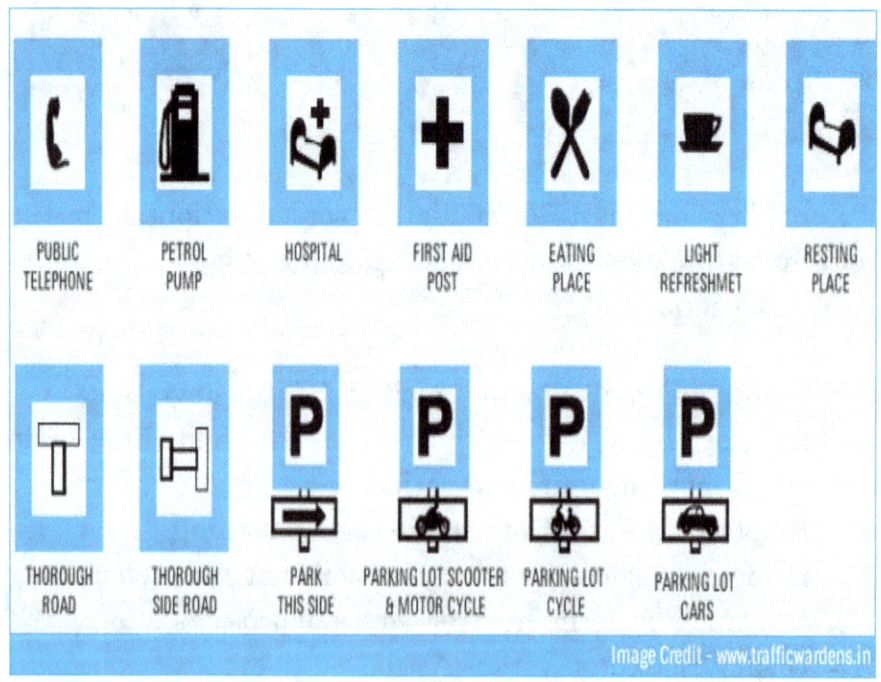

| PUBLIC TELEPHONE | PETROL PUMP | HOSPITAL | FIRST AID POST | EATING PLACE | LIGHT REFRESHMET | RESTING PLACE |

| THOROUGH ROAD | THOROUGH SIDE ROAD | PARK THIS SIDE | PARKING LOT SCOOTER & MOTOR CYCLE | PARKING LOT CYCLE | PARKING LOT CARS |

Image Credit - www.trafficwardens.in

CHAPTER 2

Think about driving on road without visuals!

CHAPTER 2

STOP
ABS
SERVICE ENGINE SOON
60 80
40
100
20
120
140
km/h
MPH
BRAKE
PS

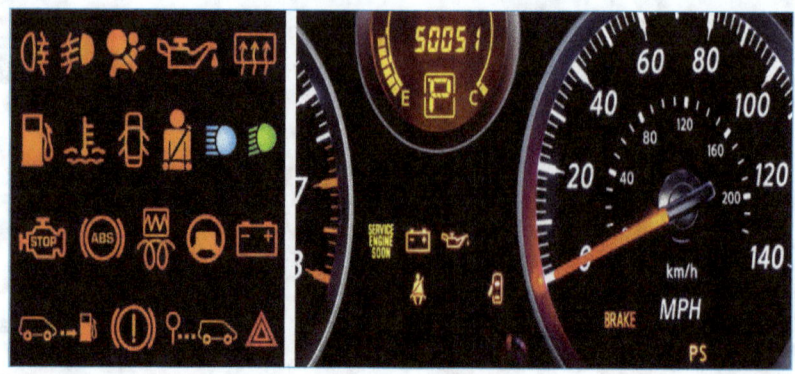

What if we get a car without these visuals?

In a nutshell, we need visuals everywhere!!!

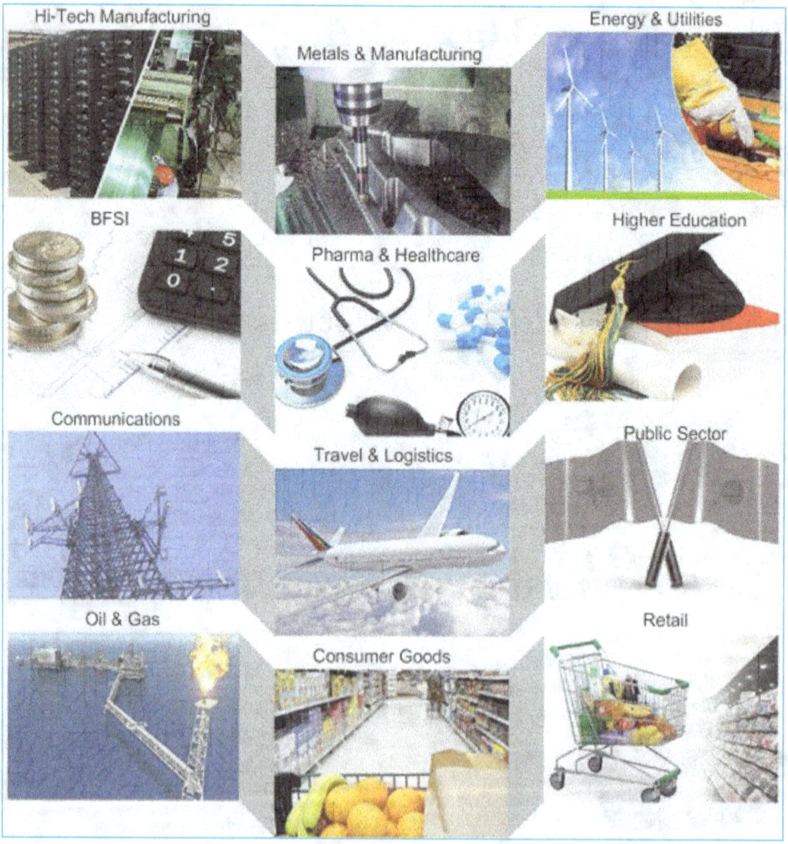
Hi-Tech Manufacturing
Metals & Manufacturing
Energy & Utilities
BFSI
Pharma & Healthcare
Higher Education
Communications
Travel & Logistics
Public Sector
Oil & Gas
Consumer Goods
Retail

KEY NOTES

- Visual Management is effective if after observing the board you can have these three scenarios clear:

  o Understand the current situation
  o Problems Exposed
  o Triggers action

- Creating a supportive environment for visual management is critical.
- Measure things against a target or standard.

QUIZ

1. **Visual boards are just for the team to view; action is to be taken only by leads in case of any deviation:**
   a. True
   b. False

2. **What information related to the team and customers can be displayed on visual boards:**
   a. All
   b. Only the information which is relevant to the overall team and within the compliance guidelines
   c. Individual information
   d. None of the above

3. **For metrics on visual boards target or standards are not compulsory**
   a. True
   b. False

4. **The aim of visual boards is to showcase about the organization to potential customers during floor visits, which helps in gaining more business**
   a. True
   b. False

5. **Aim of visual boards is to please higher management**
   a. True
   b. False

CHAPTER 2

SYSTEM THINKING

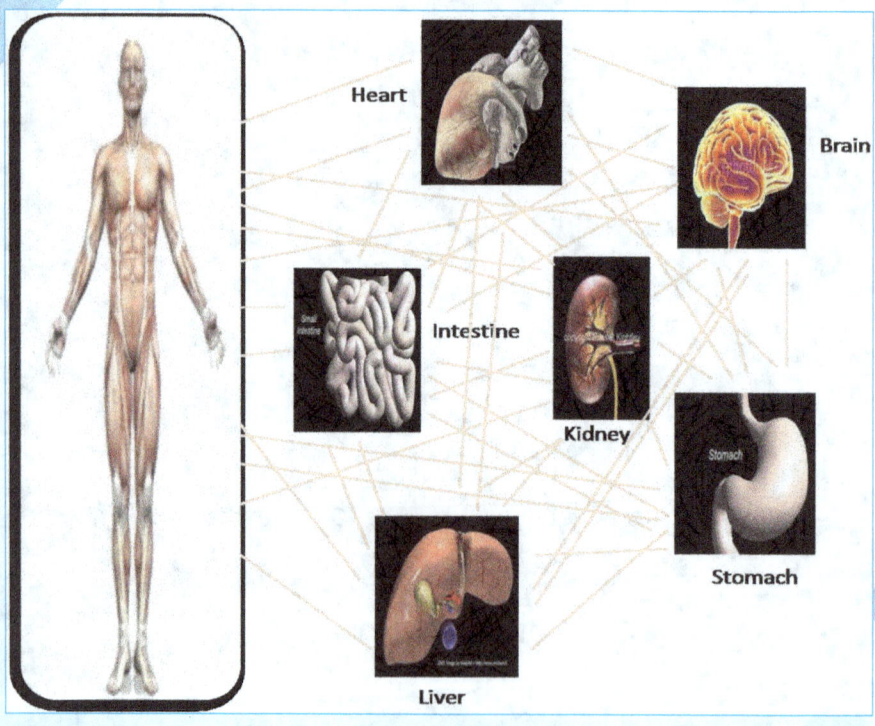

Heart

Brain

Intestine

Kidney

Stomach

Liver

The complete understanding of a system requires holistic study of not only the individual components but also their inter-linkages and the relationships with the wider system.

Whether it's medical science, manufacturing, marketing, IT, telecom or political analysis everywhere system thinking approach is required.

Frequent headaches can be the reason of some critical issues within the body. Headaches may be common in nature and something which people rarely take seriously, but higher frequency may be due to some underlying issue.

SLA breaches are the scariest metrics across organizations.

You, as the department head, are analyzing last three years of service penalties you have given to customers, for breaching SLA.

You appoint a senior member to perform the root cause analysis for the same. Interestingly, he finds that most of the penalties are from Region X. When he drills down further, he identifies that the major SLA breaches happened in the month of July and October.

Post further analysis and discussion with respective teams he establishes the root cause, *"Demand during both these months was high due to festive season in that region, and simultaneously staff availability was low"*.

For many managers this can be the accepted root cause. They will either cancel the leaves of the staff or ask them to work overtime. But it's just not the root cause... Surprised?

The festive season is just a situation, peak demands and shortage of staff can happen in any region in any month

11

irrespective of whether it's festive, seasonal, environmental change or any other exceptional reason.

Once you zero down on the months where the SLA breach is frequent, the causal analysis will start from there.

The analysis will include questions on below areas:

1. Is the team aware of this situation or not?
2. Are the team members aware of SLA targets or not?
3. Are the team members aware that missing SLA targets leads to penalty?
4. How many team members are aware of the current SLA performance of their region?
5. Do they have any daily stand-up meetings or huddles happening?
6. Are there any metrics shared with them daily?
7. In the last three months have you solved any problems specific to workplace?

If answer to any of the above is No, <u>that's the root cause</u>. And if you start addressing it, the pain will not only reduce but will also be eliminated.

Remember, if the team is aware of such serious penalties and they have staff availability board in front of them, before approving leave the leader will assess whether he has enough bandwidth to run the operation on that particular day or week, post approving these leaves.

If they have a board, where forecasted volume for the week is visible, will it not be easy for the Team Leader to plan the availability in advance?

Establishing such a process and system initially requires lots of commitment. However, once developed from top to bottom, where metrics at each layer can be visualized in such a way that every layer will work on improving and excelling on their metrics, the overall performance will improve.

For the above example, if we could have visual boards in all the regions at respective Team Leaders' level with metrics like Demand & Capacity, % Staff Availability, Backlog, etc. and targets around them, with the team simultaneously aware, empowered and motivated to take necessary action, it could have improved the metrics and performance at the respective layer.

The team can proactively plan their leaves, think of solutions to cater to the high demand during peak seasons as they are aware of the objective they have to meet and their current situation.

There are many scenarios in the real world around us where at times, we believe we have got the root cause but the reality may be different.

We may just be addressing the superficial aspect, that's the tip of an iceberg.

In the SLA breach case, the manager could have assured that people should not take leave in respective high peak months. But what if the demand pattern changes or peak months stay for long?

Breakthrough solutions and alternative approach to cater such situations can be best provided by the team on ground,

CHAPTER 3

hence enabling and empowering them with correct tools and methodologies leads to significant business improvements.

Root cause can only be ascertained if we analyze all the possible branches related to the issue.

The case was SLA breach, and the initial cause which most of us will accept is festive season and high number of leaves.

Whereas the actual reason was lack of awareness among the teams about the importance of the work they were doing and penalties paid by the department.

It's important that you address the core and not the superficial reasons.

To address the core, you have to develop the thought process of system thinking.

People, at times, put all the metrics over the wall, considering that's the best way to visual management and since one metric must be linked to the other then it's better to put all of them.

I must say that you don't need to paint your entire floor with metrics and information, and that's really not visual management, rather that's wall painting!

Remember the ground rule, any visual which does not trigger any action is just a wallpaper.

Now let's talk about some of the real-time metrics and how system thinking fits in:

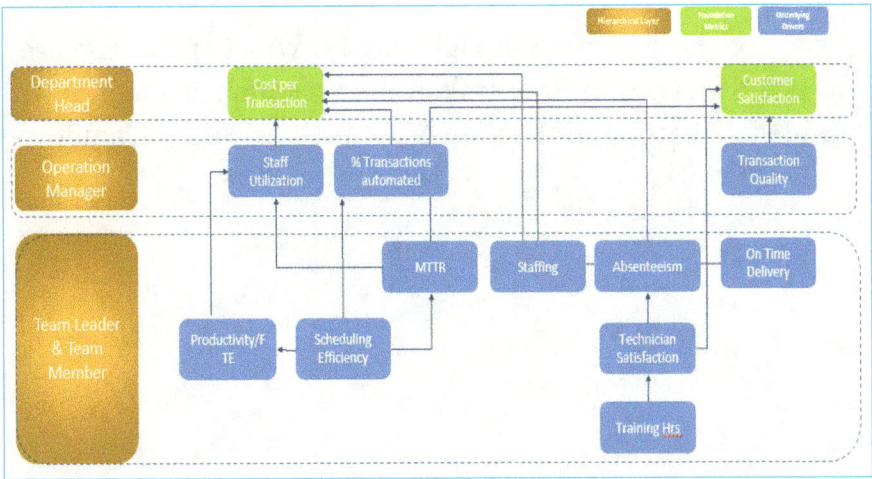

In the above illustration there are two important messages which will help us in understanding the concept clearly:

1. Hierarchical Layer – It shows the various layers within the organization and the metrics they are interested in, in other words, the focus areas for these layers. The benefits are:

   ➤ Fewer metrics to view at the respective layers
   ➤ Any deviation on metrics at the top will trigger action, which will flow down to the bottom
   ➤ All good work performed at the bottom will improve the numbers at the top

2. Linked Metrics – The way our body is connected with nerves and any issues in any of them leads to disturbances in the whole body, similarly metrics selection should be such that it provides you complete linkage with all the processes and operational touch points. How to select such metrics and find the interdependencies will be discussed in the chapter – "Identifying Metrics for Visual Management".

Both the above points are tightly coupled with each other for an effective visual management.

If we mix the layers then right action will not be triggered and if the metrics are not linked then the improvements will run in silos with no impact on critical-to-quality parameters.

KEY NOTES

- Understanding the interlinking of activities
- Metrics on visual management should have meaningful linkages with the team or department's end deliverables
- Measuring everything under the sun without any linkage only leads to confusion

QUIZ

1. System Thinking is only applicable in Healthcare:
   a. True
   b. False

2. System Thinking means understanding the interlinkage between various components and their impact on the end deliverable:
   a. True
   b. False

3. Displaying all possible metrics on the board is the best example of System Thinking:
   a. True
   b. False

4. Which approach to take to identify the metrics on visual boards based on the concept of system thinking?:
   a. Value Chain Mapping
   b. Correlation Study
   c. Ask the reporting manager
   d. A&B

5. Every layer in the organization should measure similar metrics to maintain uniformity:
   a. True
   b. False

6. Every layer in the organization should measure similar metrics to maintain uniformity:
   a. True
   b. False

7. Visual Management based on System Thinking helps in:
   a. Driving business improvement from bottom to top and vice versa
   b. Right action at right place and right time
   c. Save time in identifying the root cause
   d. All of the above

DEVELOPING MINDSET

Visual Management is not just a tool, which you would run once, get the required level of benefit then close it.

It's also not an .exe file which you double-click and a software gets installed in your and your team's desktop/laptop.

It's a culture which needs to be induced within the organization gradually, and with time it becomes the DNA of the organization.

In lean or six sigma methodology, I believe implementing visual management is really a hard nut to crack.

Putting huddle boards, getting them operational for few months in the presence of a lean consultant and then back to square one is a very common phenomenon.

Putting right visuals on boards, letting the team take ownership and interest in running them with the same level of commitment from higher management is really a complex and time consuming process.

An effective and efficient visual management requires commitment and mindset to run the same with passion.

Important factors for creating a Visual Management culture include:

- Set objectives for business
- Set goals for individual departments
- Create a plan for implementation
- Establish reasons why Visual Management is necessary
- Implement using top down approach
- Plan interactive sessions with departments
- Encourage participation and ownership

SET OBJECTIVES FOR BUSINESS

Before implementation begins, the leadership needs to define the organization's expectations regarding visual management.

These leaders need to fully understand how the use of visual management contributes to the overall goals of the company.

The diagram here clearly shows how the organization's goal is interlinked with respective department's objective and employees' objectives.

If these objectives are not mapped with each other, then the overall organization goals will be difficult to achieve.

Hence, it's the responsibility of the leaders to set the objectives in alignment to organization goals.

> *"A mere 7% of employees today fully understand their company's business strategies and what's expected of them in order to help achieve company goals."*

Robert S. Kaplan and David P. Norton, "The Strategy-Focused Organization," Harvard Business School Press, 2001

SET GOALS FOR INDIVIDUAL DEPARTMENTS

Every department must have a different set of goals and dynamics. It's important that we understand these dynamics and set goals in context to department's environment, expectations and how the department deliverables are linked to organization's goal.

CREATE A PLAN FOR IMPLEMENTATION

For the business goals to be met, proper organizational mindset must be cultivated.

This collective mindset acts as a foundation for the power and creativity of visual management.

For visual communication to flourish, information needs to be made available to everyone.

CHAPTER 4

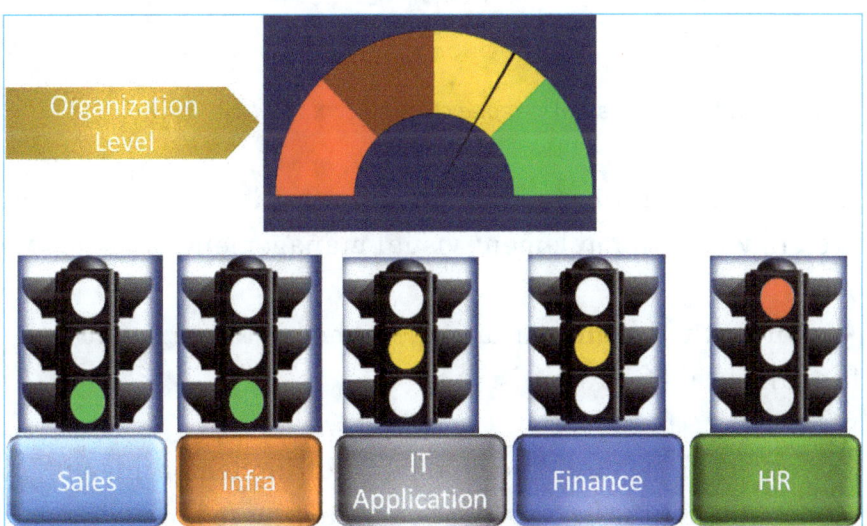

An effective visual management process drives productivity, quality and innovative spirit of each department, which in turn fuels the growth of the organization.

ESTABLISH REASONS WHY VISUAL MANAGEMENT IS NECESSARY

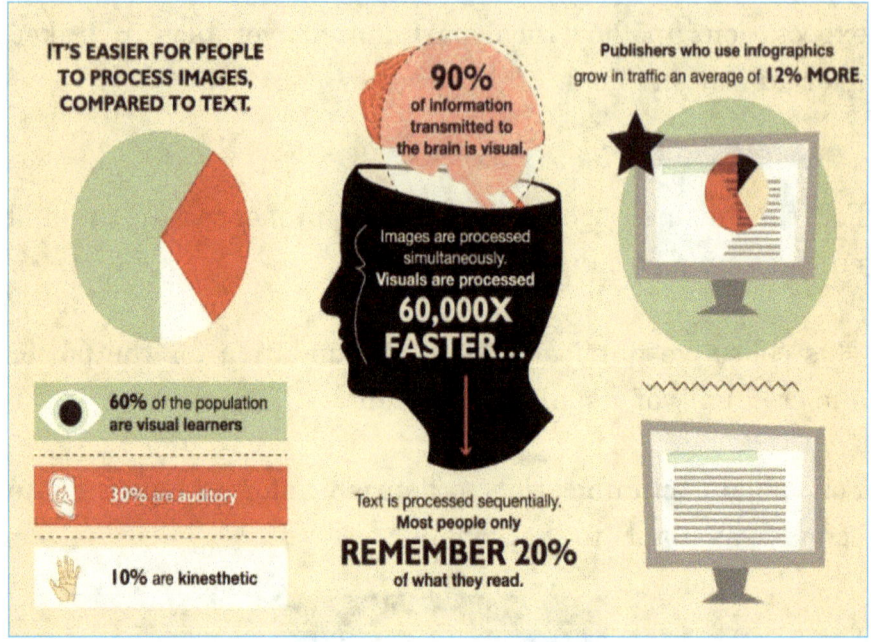

Image Courtesy - https://venngage.com/blog/marketing-psychology/

It is best to build a strong foundation by defining the initial area in which to implement visual management.

As with other Lean initiatives, it helps to start with the fundamental 5S practices.

As you develop more specific tactics for implementing visual management, it is best to focus on areas where large amounts of information need to be exchanged.

Employees need to feel that they actually need visual management tools if they are expected to use them.

CHAPTER 4

It is important to create an environment where employees truly desire process improvement, before bombarding them with performance evaluations and metrics.

IMPLEMENT USING TOP DOWN APPROACH

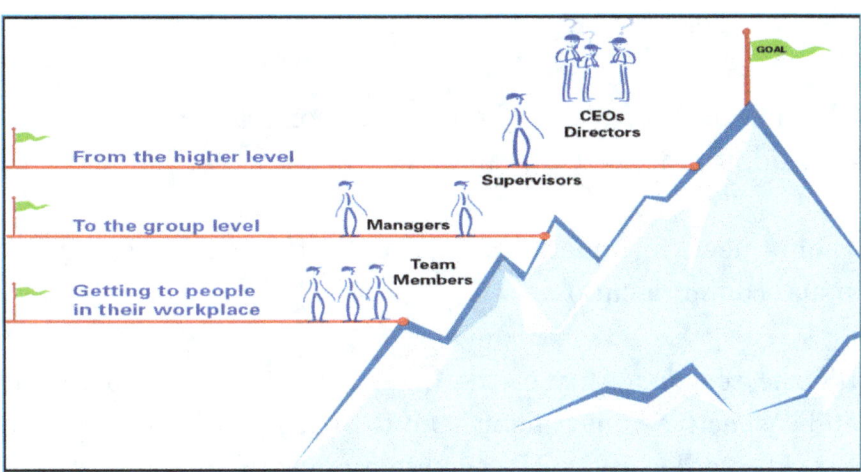

Image Courtesy - http://planet-lean.com/how-to-create-an-effective-daily-management-system

There is a saying "Practice what you preach".

This saying is quite relevant in implementing visual management. In most of the organizations, visual management fails because of the lack of focus from top leadership.

An updated visual board of the CEO/director will trigger action; any action triggered from the higher level will flow down to the group level, and simultaneously to the team members' level.

Hence, it becomes crucial for top leadership to have real-time view of key performances and that too on clearly visible boards. Focusing on visualization will allow everyone to see the powerful effects of visual management.

CHAPTER 4

PLAN INTERACTIVE SESSIONS WITH DEPARTMENTS

Most experts recommend starting with a small model of visual management.

It is best to give visual management culture the time and support it needs to develop.

The mindset of visual communication cannot be forced. Instead, it must be cultivated.

Teams need to understand the importance and benefits of visual communication.

It's the responsibility of the business excellence consultant and respective department head to engage with the team, be part of huddles and make them more interactive.

Image Courtesy - https://entegy.com.au/executing-the-perfect-interactive-session/

CHAPTER 4

ENCOURAGE PARTICIPATION AND OWNERSHIP BY DEPARTMENTS

Huddles over visual boards should be interactive, full of fun and objective based.

Everyone should be encouraged to participate in the creation of rules and standards.

Monitoring processes should never be seen as simply a way to blame individuals.

Information displayed should be recognized as a means of solving problems for the greater good of the organization.

Ideas and feedbacks must be taken during any situation from team members.

Action items arising out of a situation on visual boards must be equally distributed among team members.

The facilitator of daily huddle must be rotated to induce the sense of accountability and ownership.

CHAPTER 4

KEY NOTES

- Visual management is not a onetime run tool, it's a culture which needs to be practiced with commitment, and be gradually induced within the entire organization.
- Visual management cannot be forced to practice.
- Top leadership commitment is a critical success factor for efficient and effective visual management.
- It's an approach to make people participate in the business/operational excellence journey.
- Teams must be trained and encouraged to practice visual management.
- Make visual management fun, to increase its adaptability.
- Visual boards must be made lively and interesting.

QUIZ

1. The 1st step you take while implementing visual management:
   a. Set objectives clears for the business
   b. Set goals for individual departments
   c. Create a plan for organization-wide implementation
   d. Establish reasons for why visual management is necessary

2. Why you need goals for individual departments?:
   a. To please the higher management
   b. To be audit compliant
   c. To ensure department's focus on its goals and plan the governance plan accordingly
   d. All of the above

3. Why is it recommended to implement visual management using Top Down approach?:
   a. Visual management is a practice which requires commitment hence leaders need to lead by example
   b. Deviation of metrics from target at top will lead to cascading of right concerns to the right department for action
   c. Higher management is more skilled
   d. A & B

4. Why is it necessary to establish a reason for "Why Visual Management is necessary?"
   a. For CMMI certification
   b. To convince and engage people across the organization to be more participative, and harness its benefits
   c. A & B
   d. Only B

5. Why is it necessary to engage team members in interactive sessions before implementing visual management?
   a. For better understanding of its objectives
   b. For encouraging more participation and inducing interest
   c. To make them aware how visual management works
   d. To make them understand it's not forced on them
   e. All of the above

IDENTIFYING METRICS FOR VISUAL BOARDS

We have seen in our previous chapters, how we need to think holistically while implementing visual management. We have also seen the deployment approach of top down, and working on the mindset to ensure that visual management works effectively.

Now once you have decided to implement visual management across your organization, the key question that will arise is 'What to show on the visual?' 'How can we ensure that the visuals are effective and aligned to the objective?' 'How to identify the metrics for visual management?'

In this chapter, which is the most critical part of this book, we will discuss how one can identify metrics for visuals. You will find certain terminologies related to six sigma, which have been briefly explained in this book.

Before we start, let us refer back to the chapter "Developing a Visual Management Mindset". We have mentioned "*Every department has a different set of goals and dynamics. It's important to understand these dynamics and set goals in the context of the department's environment, expectations and how the department's deliverables are linked to the organization's goals.*"

The above text basically sets the context of identifying metrics. The visual board must measure items which are related to the department goals, and any deviation of these metrics from the target will impact achieving the overall goal.

Translate the goals and objectives into metrics.

Customer needs or organization's goals can be translated to Critical to Quality Parameters, and then these CTQs can be broken down into Critical to Process (CTPs).

If you improve your CTPs, your CTQs will automatically improve which will impact your customer's satisfaction level and ensure that your organization's goals are met.

How it works?

Think about a machine, where you put raw material inside and you get processed product as the output.

If your raw material's quality is good, then your overall product's quality will also be good.

CHAPTER 5

If you start putting garbage inside, then definitely the product will have multiple deformities.

CTQ is the output of the process, whereas CTPs are the inputs to the process. If you control your inputs and work well on them, you definitely will get a quality output.

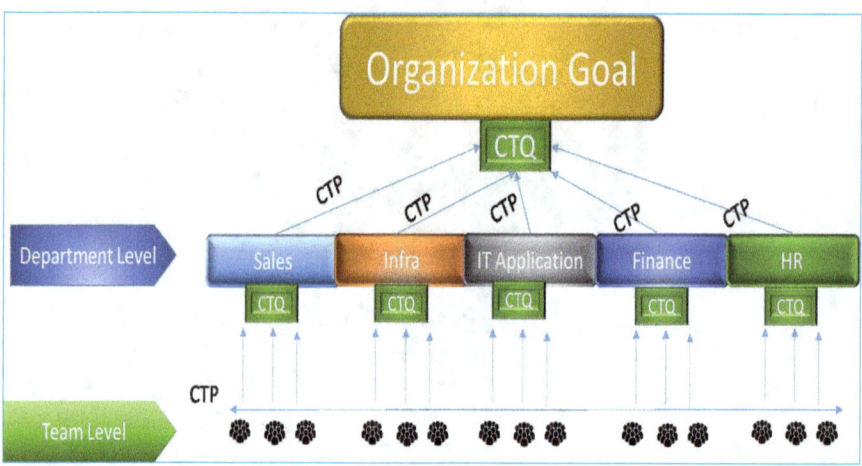

This structure explains that every layer has its own CTQs and CTPs and they are tightly coupled with each other. Disturbance in the performance of any layer in the entire value chain will lead to impact the overall goals.

Let's study an example of CTQs and CTPs in a Service Desk environment which will give more clarity.

In a Service Desk, a customer wants <1% abandonment rate (no. of calls going unanswered) and 95% CSAT.

CTQs

1. Abandonment Rate – <1%
2. CSAT – 95%

CTPs

1. Productivity/FTE
2. Call Quality Score
3. Average Handling Time
4. %Attrition
5. %Unplanned Leaves
6. %Availability on AUX

There can be more such CTPs depending on the environment.

If CTPs perform well then the CTQs will definitely be in a better shape. The CTPs can be further broken down at different levels for monitoring.

e.g. Productivity/FTE can be viewed at the visual board of Operation Manager whereas AHT and After Call Work Time can be the key parameters for Team Leaders and Team Members' Visual Board.

Identifying the right CTPs is really important. There must be a correlation with the parameter which we have identified as CTP of a CTQ.

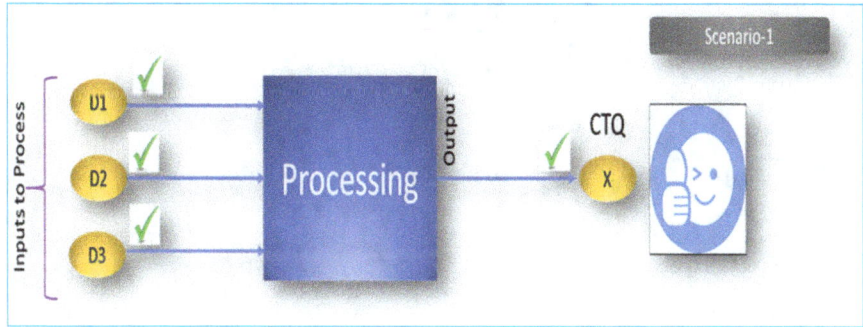

1. CTPs linked to CTQs
2. CTPs performing as expected

3. CTQ on target
4. Happy Customer

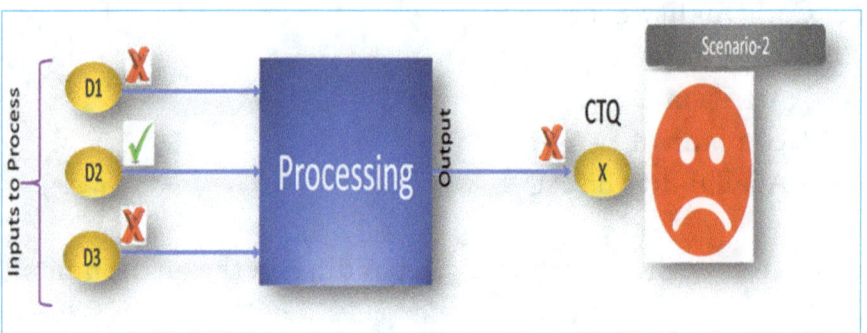

1. CTPs linked to CTQs
2. CTPs not performing as expected
3. CTQ missing the target
4. Dissatisfied Customer

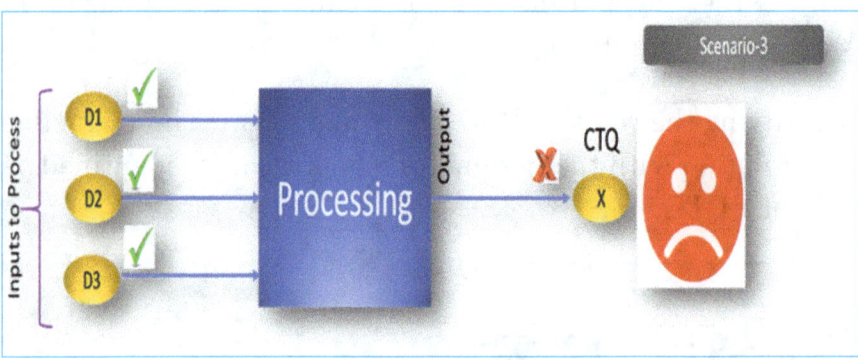

1. CTPs performing as expected
2. CTQ missing the target
3. Dissatisfied Customer

Let us see what's wrong in this scenario. All the input parameters to process are perfect yet the Critical To Quality aspect is not on target.

It's because the CTPs identified here are not at all correlated with the CTQ.

We will see the practical aspect of this correlation factor post scenario – 4.

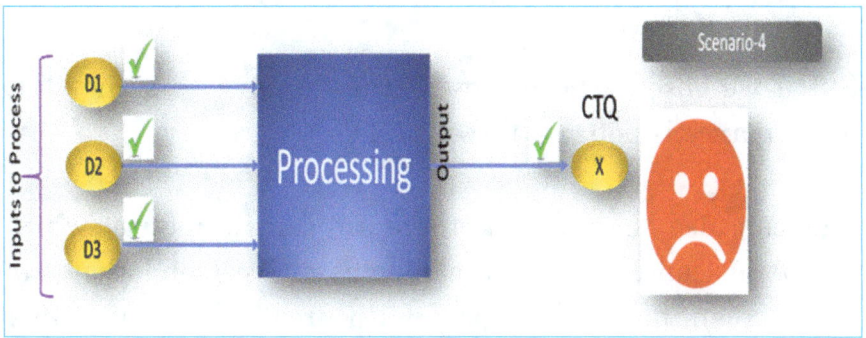

1. CTPs performing as expected
2. CTQ on target
3. Dissatisfied Customer

Wow!! Now this is interesting. This scenario is observed in many projects, where leaders at times measure certain things which are nowhere related to customer's requirement. For them, they are meeting the metrics they assumed as the key quality parameters, yet the customer is unhappy.

Scenario 3 & Scenario 4 are pretty common. At times each department has its own objectives and works in silos, these objectives are entirely different from the organization's objectives.

Each department has its dashboard in green, but at the top, the CEO's dashboard is in dark RED.

Hence, it's important that objectives are linked and metrics are tightly coupled with the objectives.

For all of us, Scenario -1 and Scenario – 2 are normal and as per the six sigma concept if your CTPs are performing good, your CTQs will also be perfect and vice versa.

But if we observe Scenario - 3 and Scenario – 4, the CTQ performance is not in sync with CTPs.

This can also be viewed as there are certain metrics which are being captured at team members' level and they are all in green, but the metrics which are captured at higher management level are in red and vice versa.

Now the question arises, if this is the scenario how can the chain effect be created and how can positive work done at the bottom level not get reflected at the top?

Remember the chapter "System Thinking"? Yes, the same system thinking is to be applied while you select metrics on visual boards and performance hubs.

There should be mapping and strong relationship between these metrics and your performance.

Hence, the identified CTPs will only be correct, when they are in direct correlation with the CTQs statistically.

We will see some of the examples and see how the concept of correlation plays a big role while identifying metrics.

In my previous example, where a team had identified two CTQs:

1. Abandonment Rate – <1%
2. CSAT – 95%

We will see the correlation aspect of it with various CTPs.

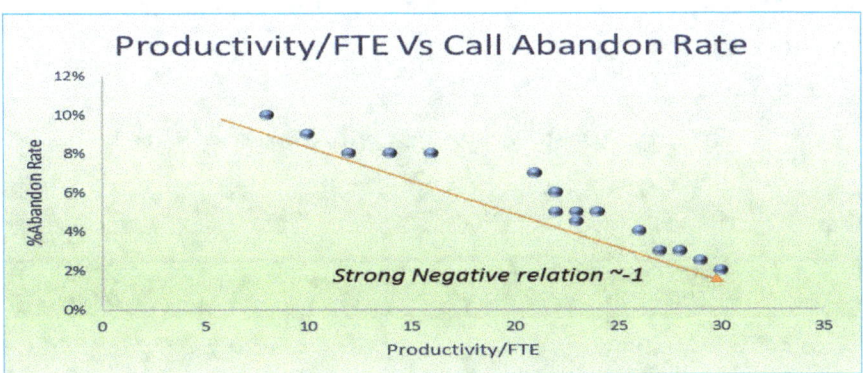

Higher the productivity/FTE, lower the abandonment rate, as the team strives to create more capacity for themselves to take calls.

Even the relationship co-efficient is -1, which shows a strong negative relationship.

Let's see another one.

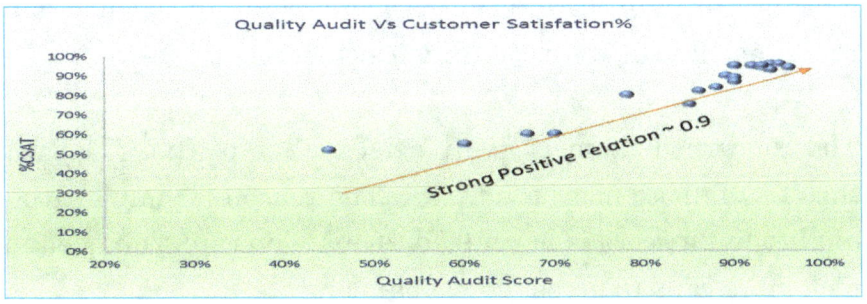

Higher the Quality Audit score, better the Customer Satisfaction.

The relationship co-efficient is ~1, which shows strong positive relationship.

Let's see the example which we studied in Scenario – 3 earlier in this chapter.

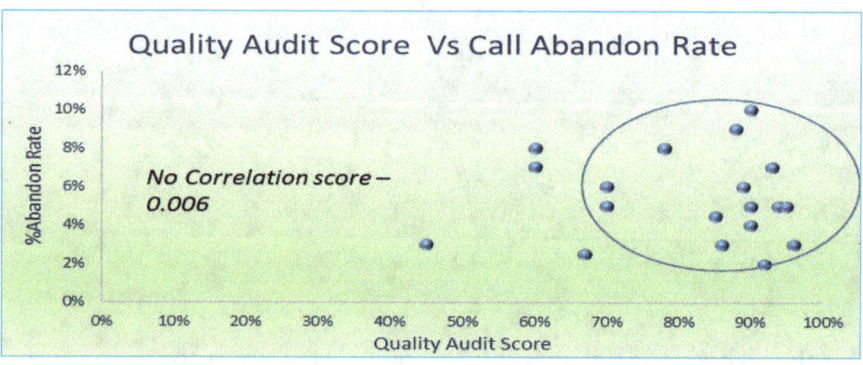

% Abandon Rate is directly related to Productivity/FTE, if advisors pick more calls you will have more capacity to handle calls, hence your abandon rate will go down.

But think of a scenario where the Team leader is aggressively performing Call Quality Audit and his audit score is about 95%, higher than the internal target of 90%, yet the abandon rate breaches the agreed SLA with customers.

The concerned team is doing good on one of the CTPs yet the CTQ fails to meet the target. The reason is simple, good quality audit score is not linked to abandon rate, you need to pick more calls to arrest your abandon rate.

In the above graph, the correlation score is 0.006 which shows that there exists no relation between Quality Audit Score and Abandon Rate.

Remember, these relationships between parameters may vary from account to account. We are just taking these examples for understanding purpose.

You can refer the below image to calculate the correlation between two parameters in excel

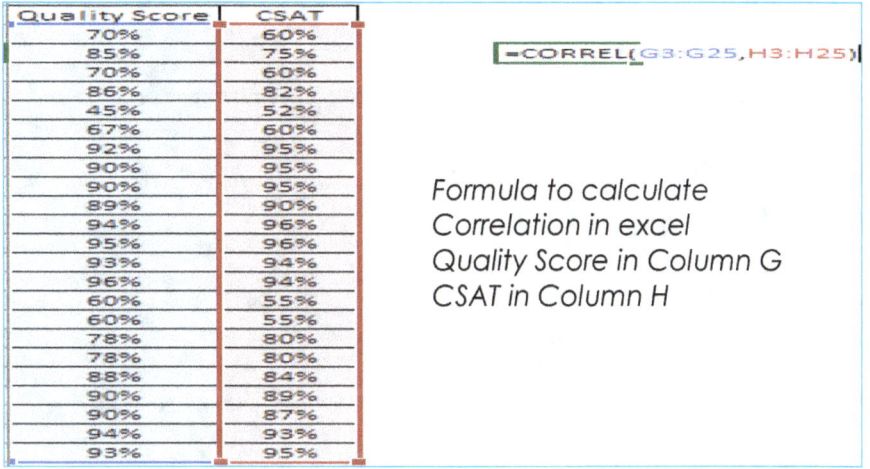

While deciding metrics for your own team or department, it's very important to understand the objective.

So ask a few questions:

1. What's your team/department's objective?
2. What is the critical success factor?
3. How my performance is linked to the end objective?
4. What are my customer touch points?
5. What all work we as a team perform?

6. Why am I measuring this?
7. What if this metric is in red?
8. Do I have a defined target for all the metrics?
9. Do my metrics have any relationship with customers/ organization goals?

Too many measurements are not good, rather they make the floor confused and derive no value for you.

KEY NOTES
- Every department must understand their objective and customer (Internal/External) requirements/organization's objectives.
- They need to translate the objective in to measurable terms called CTQs (Critical to Quality).
- CTQs need to further break down in to CTPs (Critical to Process)
- CTPs measured must have strong relationship with CTQs.
- Use Scatter charts and correlations to identify the metrics.
- Visual Boards should have key CTQs and CTPs in place.

QUIZ

1. **Why Objective Mapping is necessary for individual teams with that of the organization:**
   a. To form a complete value chain
   b. So that appraisal hikes can be decided
   c. To ensure that the entire organization is working towards meeting the organization's objectives
   d. To ensure that the team feels more accountable of their work
   e. A, B, C, D
   f. A, C, D

2. **CTQ can only be provided by the customer:**
   a. True
   b. False

3. **Ensuring that CTQs meet the target is more important than the associated CTPs**
   a. True
   b. False

4. **CTQs and CTPs are a classic example of**
   a. System Thinking
   b. Value Addition
   c. Waste in process
   d. All of the above

5. **Correlation value of -0.7 between 2 metrics means:**
   a. Metrics are not correlated
   b. Metrics are directly proportional to each other
   c. Metrics are inversely proportional to each other
   d. Strong positive relationship

6. **Correlation value of 0.7 between 2 metrics means:**
   a. Metrics are not correlated
   b. Metrics are directly proportional to each other
   c. Metrics are inversely proportional to each other
   d. Strong negative relationship

7. **Correlation value of 0.02 between 2 metrics means:**
   a. Metrics are not correlated
   b. Strong positive relationship
   c. Strong negative relationship
   d. None of the above

CHAPTER 5

PERFORMANCE HUBS

In this chapter, we will see how the designed visuals can help in running performance hubs at respective layers and induce a culture of continuous improvement and ownership among team members.

The Objective of Performance Hub: To enable everyone to immediately see deviations from the optimum state of work and working, and to enable immediate corrective action.

As I mentioned earlier as well, if any visual does not trigger any action then it's just a wallpaper or a story board.

The measurement on your visual hubs should be such that it triggers action, if anything deviates from its set target.

A routine discussion on the visual boards will convert them into performance hubs.

The discussion needs to be concise, targeted and action-oriented.

We will discuss in detail how to set up the performance hubs and ensure their success.

A Performance Hub provides a mechanism for teams to visualize and review performance and agree on right actions to deliver improvement.

Below are two types of boards used in organizations:

A Physical Board

https://www.thedsmgroup.com

A virtual team dashboard reviewed through 'live meeting' or similar application

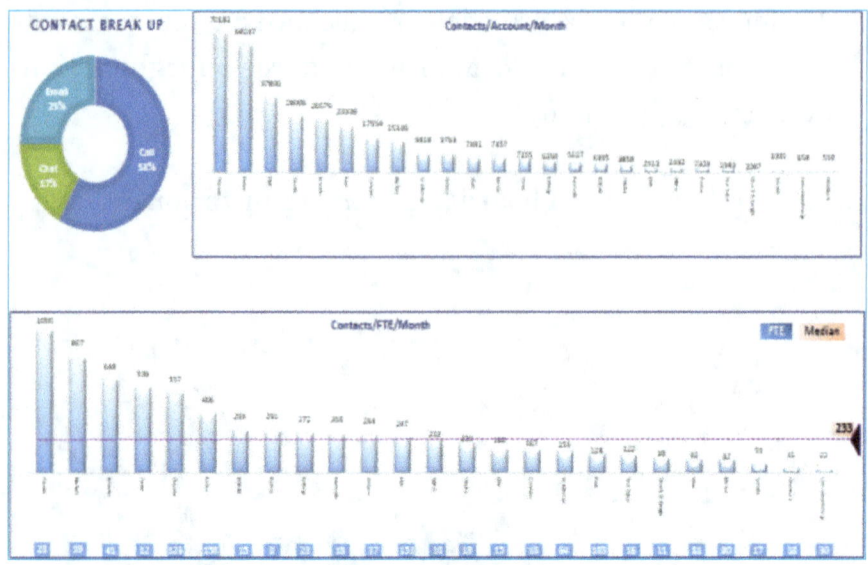

Yes, the participation of a team is crucial from top to bottom to ensure the success of visual management and performance hubs.

Benefits:

- Improved teamwork and focus on KPIs.
- Visual indication of performance and position within bigger picture.

- It is an opportunity to discuss improvements and gain consensus.
- Focusing on team objectives on a day-to-day basis accelerates performance improvement.
- Teams energized and performing to their full potential, achieving their targets, form a much happier environment to work than a team that's failing to meet its objectives.

Performance Hub Layout

Objectives	Situation	Complication	Resolution	Recognition
Objective	Metrics	Concern	Quick Fix / Practical Problem Solving	Key Success / Star Of the Month

Sections Description:

Objective – Irrespective of which layer's performance hub we are laying out, it's very important to have objectives section, so that people can relate their work with the objective of the team, department and the organization. As we discussed in our previous chapter "Identifying Metrics" we saw that clarity around objectives is very crucial. You can only think of measuring something when you have a goal around it. The answer to questions like, what to measure for effective visual management and performance enhancement, is to have your objectives defined in the first place.

Situation –

Situation is the measurement section where you need to put in your daily/weekly/monthly measures, ensure to have target against every measure, so that right action can be triggered at the right time.

Complication –

Any metric deviating from its targeted state will move to the complication stage. You will have a specific space in your hub which records your complications arising out of your situation. This will ensure that the team discusses and works on complications.

Resolution –

In this section, the action plan and resolution of the complications is to be provided. This helps in giving visibility about what complications we have and what all complications have resolutions in progress.

Recognition –

It's always said in the lean methodology "Celebrate every success". The person or the team that has successfully resolved a complication has their names highlighted in this section.

Any customer appreciation, higher management appreciation or exceptional target achievement needs to be in the Recognition section. The team needs to feel a sense of pride and achievement so the recognition section needs to be designed accordingly.

OBJECTIVE MAPPING

Translation of organizational objectives to individual objectives with complete end to end mapping.

CHAPTER 6

It provides an individual with the understanding of how important his/her job is and how their individual effort is making a difference at the organization level.

By performing this exercise, you are connecting the entire organization to one goal and driving the overall organization to meet the goals.

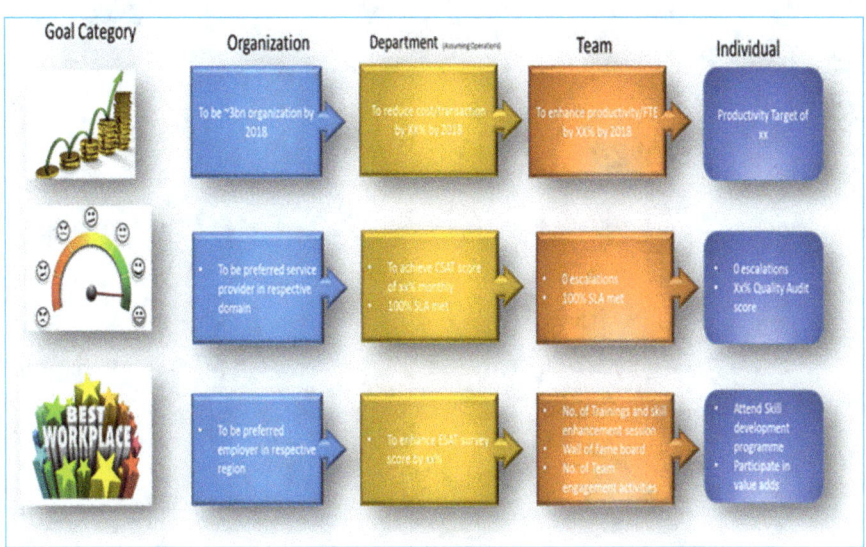

SITUATION MAPPING

As discussed earlier, the situation section is all about how you perform against your objectives. So the situation for the department head will be against the objectives of the department. Similarly, for Operations lead/Manager leave will be against the objective of the team.

Let's see how a team's situation will look like based on the objectives we have seen earlier.

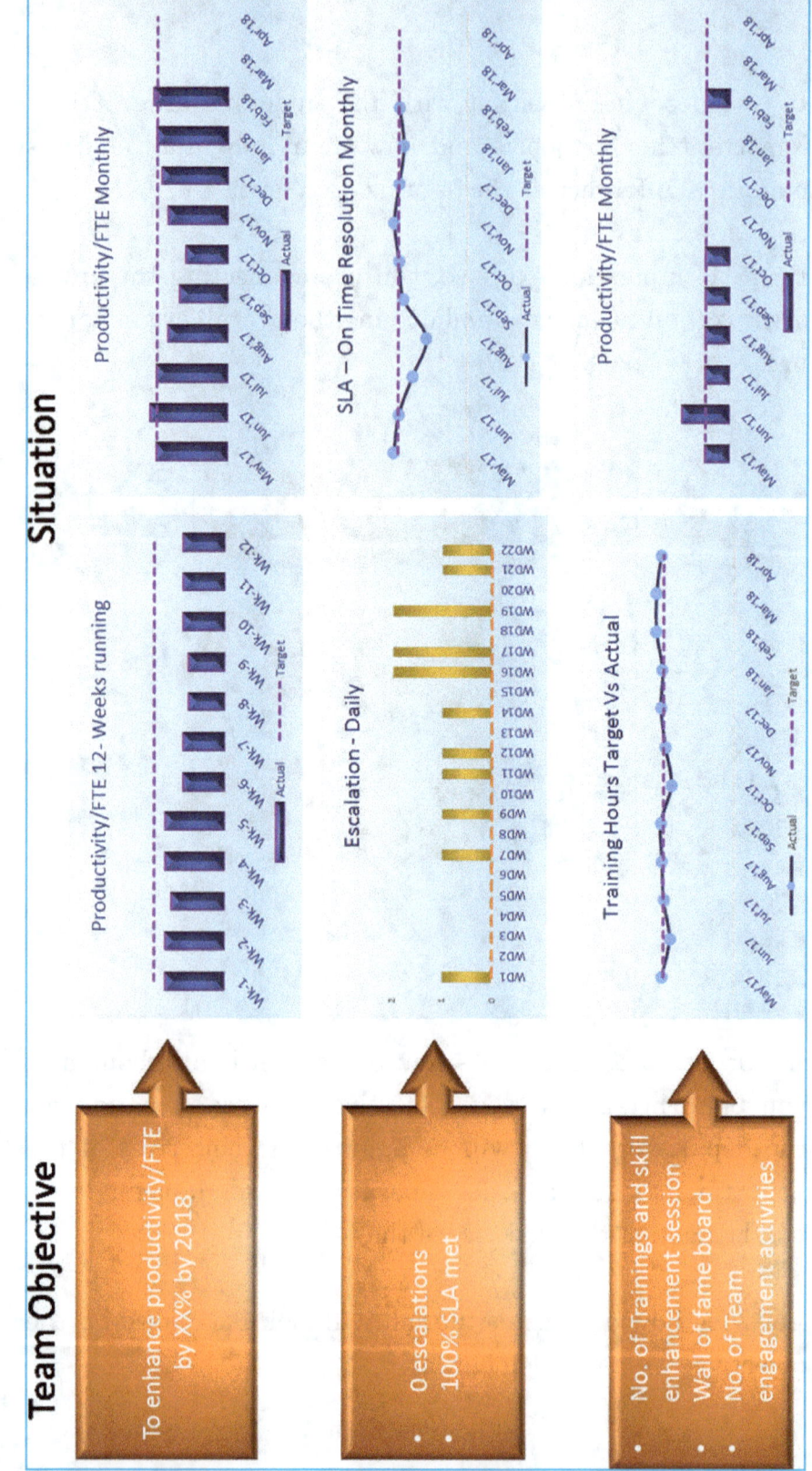

In this entire situation part, few things are important to note:

1. All measures are derived from the objective.
2. All measures have a defined target, as nothing can be triggered as action if you don't have any target.
3. There are daily, weekly, and monthly cuts of measures, the measurement frequency is critical. A high impacting metric needs to be measured daily to keep a close tab.

COMPLICATION MAPPING

Complication - In this section, you need to derive the concerns triggering out of a situation. Remember this chain is crucial, your situation is derived from the objectives, and your complication should be derived from your situation.

Let's see how a team's complication will look like based on the situation we have seen earlier.

RESOLUTION MAPPING

In this section, you need to resolve the concerns you have identified from the complication.

Let's see how a team's resolution will look like based on the complication we have seen earlier.

RECOGNITION MAPPING

We will elaborate more on the 5C approach in the next chapter, as an effective Visual Management needs strong problem solving methodology.

In this section, you need to resolve the concerns you have identified from the complication.

Let's see how a team's recognition will look like based on the resolution we have seen earlier.

CHAPTER 6

47

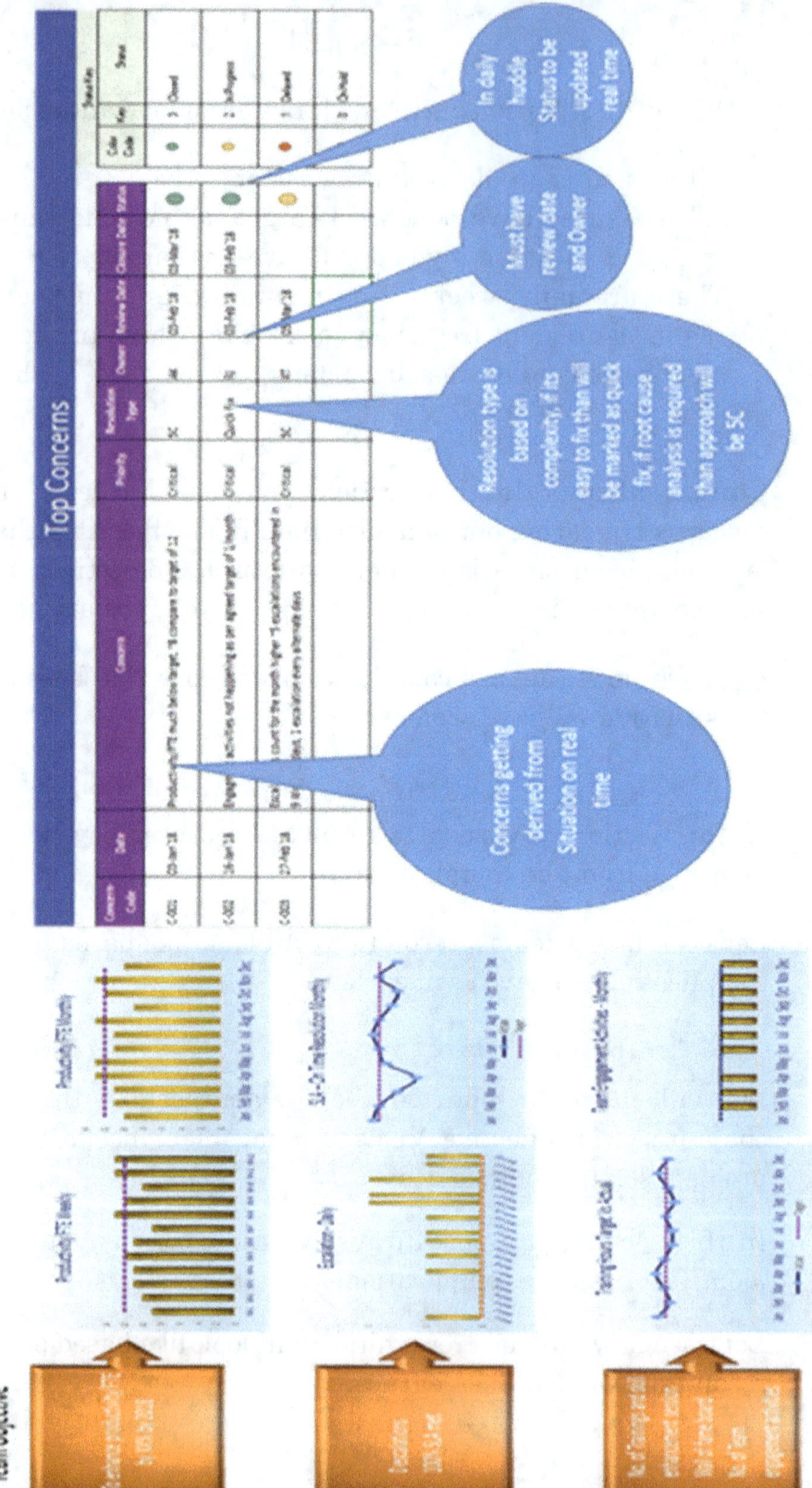

Resolution

Complication

CHAPTER 6

PPS - SC

Concern Code	Date	Concern	Containment	Cause	Correction	Planned Closure	Actual Closure Date	Owner	Status
C-001	10-Oct'18	Productivity PTS much below the target. It compare to target of 5	NA	Ticket related to server are taking long time to resolve, with only 30% resources well versed. Hands on to be provided to 70% of resources	Resolution document to be prepared. Session on Server resolution and hands on to be provided to 70% of resources	01-Mar'18	05-May'18	AK	
C-003	01-Feb'18	Escalations count for the month higher. 3 escalations encountered in 9 working days, 1 escalation every alternate days	NA	3 out of 5 escalations are related to closure of customer query without prior confirmation	Awareness email to be triggered if score is not resolved, ticket cannot be closed till customer click on "Yes" button	05-Apr'18		SGT	

Status Key

Concern Identified	0	
Root cause Identified	1	
Solution Identified	2	
Solution Implementation - In Progress	3	
Solution Implemented - Benefit realized	4	

Top Concerns

Recognition

Key Success

Sr. No	Date	Success	Benefits: (Quantified)	Other Benefits	Lesson Learnt
1	03-Mar'18	Productivity/FTE average improved from 8 to 11.5	43% improvement in Productivity leading to higher resolution of tickets and reduction in inventory	NA	Best Practice and SOP documents to be shared among wider team

Star Of The Month

Sr. No	Month	Star Of the Month	Achievement
1	Jan'18	Arvind Kumar	Identified root cause behind low productivity/FTE
2	Feb'18	Rahul J	Efforts in ensuring engagement activities performed monthly as per planned

Resolution

PDCA

We have seen an illustration, view of how team hubs look like. Let us now focus on the Hub layout.

From the illustration we have seen how every section of the hub is linked to each other. If we follow the core concept as it is then it will help in meeting the overall team objective.

It works on the concept of Pull, where every section pulls out its action from the previous section and at the end we derive value for the team and the organization.

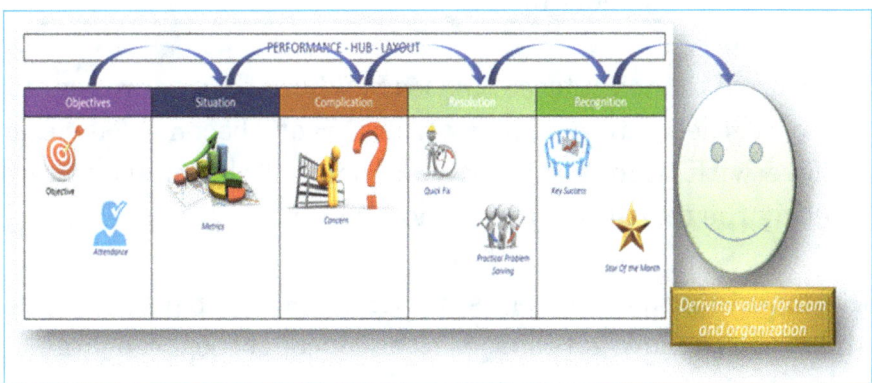

From the above image, it's evident how each section of the performance hub is linked to each other and delivers value to the organization. Most important is the team effort that is proactive in nature and perfectly aligned to the objectives.

All the positive work done at the bottom layer will have a ripple effect at the top.

Points to Note:

1. Situation section of the performance hub must be derived from the objectives.
2. Each metric must have realistic targets associated to it.

3. Concerns must be pulled up from the situation once you observe that your metrics are not meeting the target.

4. It may happen that in a given month you won't have any concerns, but if the concerns are frequent then you need to review your situation and objectives sections based on the below questionnaire:

   ➢ Are my objectives correctly aligned to the organization's objectives?
   ➢ Are my situations correlated with the objectives?
   ➢ Are we measuring the things rightly?
   ➢ Are the targets too low?

Majority of the team faces this issue where they get reluctant to revise their targets, hence the targets become easier to achieve with time. Gradually, majority of the metrics start meeting the target, leading to no concern.

It's important that the teams challenge their own performance and revise their targets based on the concept of best repeatable. Once the teams get into that mode, they keep on identifying innovative ways to achieve more accuracy and efficiency.

Hub Meeting Rules:

- Hub's relevant sections to be kept updated
- Hub meeting time should remain fixed
- Hub meeting at team level should not exceed more than 15 minutes
- Hub meeting at team level should occur daily
- Department level hub meeting can be weekly
- Hub meeting time for department level can be 30-60 minutes
- Team level hub meeting to be attended by Team Leader/ Ops Manager and all resources of the respective team

- Department level hub meeting to be attended by Team Lead/Ops Manager of respective teams within the department and respective Department Heads
- CEO level hub meeting to be attended by CEO and all department heads

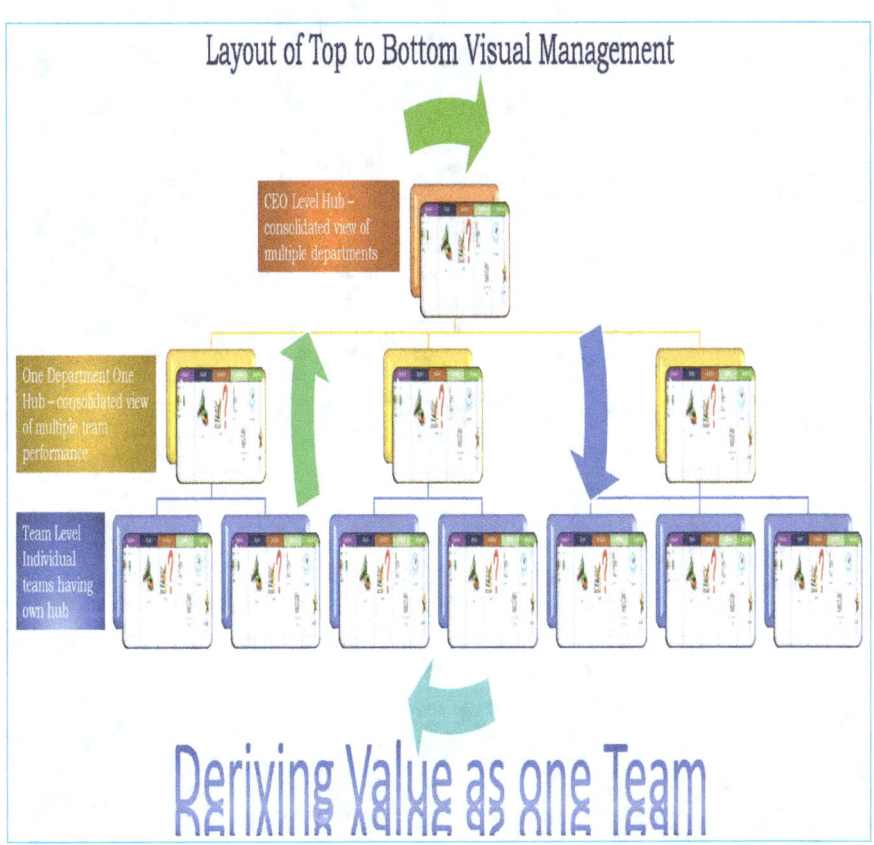

KEY NOTES

- Resolution – Concerns based on the complexity to be resolved either as quick fix or using 5C methodology.
- Recognition – Highlight your success and star achiever of the month in this section, to motivate your team about all the great work they are putting in.
- Targets around metrics to be realistic and SMART. Too low targets will lead to lethargic way of working and will not trigger innovative approach in the team.
- Best repeatable method is also suitable in deciding the targets.
- Performance hubs should look lively, hence use of colors is recommended.
- Performance hubs can also be electronic to conduct a smooth session with cross-located team members.
- Department heads and CEOs also need to conduct their hub meetings; to ensure that they are also playing an active role in the value chain.

CHAPTER 6

QUIZ

1. **Performance hubs can only be**
   a. Electronic
   b. Physical Boards
   c. Both Physical and Electronic
   d. Either a or b

2. **Metrics in Situation section need to be derived from:**
   a. Complications
   b. Objectives
   c. Based on Manager's recommendation
   d. Both a & c

3. Department head should not attend Operations Level Performance hub meeting:
   a. True
   b. False

4. Department head's performance hub to have all the metrics measured across all the teams within the department:
   a. True
   b. False

5. For a team hub within a department, the objective section must have objectives linked to:
   a. Organization's Objectives
   b. Department's Objectives
   c. Both a and b
   d. Team leader's objective

6. For a department's hub within an organization the objective section must have objectives linked to:
   a. Organization's Objectives
   b. Department's Objectives
   c. Both a and b
   d. Department's head objective

7. Situation section must have the following:
   a. Metrics linked to Objectives
   b. Daily/Weekly and Monthly Trends of Identified Metrics
   c. Targets/Standards for Each Metric
   d. All of the above

8. Situation Section must have the top concerns:
   a. True
   b. False

9. Complication Section derives itS input from:
   a. Objective
   b. Situation
   c. Resolution
   d. None of the above

CHAPTER 6

10. If there are no concerns in the Complication section yet the customer is unhappy that shows:
    a. Metrics are not correctly aligned to the customer needs/objectives
    b. Targets are too low for respective metrics
    c. Measurement system is not correct
    d. All of the above

11. A concern which is not getting pulled out from the Situation section cannot be a part of the Complication section:
    a. True
    b. False

12. Resolution section is derived from:
    a. Recognition
    b. Situation
    c. Complication
    d. Objective

13. Resolution section is not mandatory for performance hub:
    a. True
    b. False

14. Recognition section is not mandatory for performance hub:
    a. True
    b. False

15. Recognition section is derived from:
    a. Resolution
    b. Situation
    c. Complication
    d. Objective

16. A performance hub must only use the following naming convention "Objective", "Situation", "Complication" and "Resolution":
    a. True
    b. False

17. **The section which boosts healthy team competition and morale of the team members:**
    a. Resolution
    b. Situation
    c. Recognition
    d. Objective

PROBLEM SOLVING METHODOLOGY (5C)

In the last chapter, we studied how to design visual boards and then run them as the performance hub.

We have also seen how these hubs can be configured at every layer across the organization, and a significant level of commitment is required to gain benefits from them.

We also studied about the various sections in the hub which can be named accordingly, it is important to keep the concept alive.

In this chapter, we will discuss about the entire concept of visual management that can shift the team's mindset from firefighting to proactive mode.

We always see concerns and challenges around workplace. At times, people put their efforts to resolve them, but without any methodical approach, the problems re-occur, and by that time the person who resolved it previously is not part of the team anymore. So the entire team starts the analysis and problem resolution from scratch.

There are various scenarios where you definitely need to have strong problem-solving methodology.

Scenario - 1

There is a concern within the team, which the team is aware of, but is ignoring it and treating it as a BAU, as few in the team feel it unnecessary to raise the issue when they have a temporary fix in place.

One day, the issue re-occurs as usual but the temporary fix does not work. The customer gets impacted, the entire team goes into firefighting mode to resolve the same.

Scenario - 2

Suman is a senior resource in a team and it's his responsibility to resolve any concern on the performance board. Suman met with an emergency situation and will not be available for the next three months. Now the team leader is under stress as the multiple concerns that Suman was responsible for are creating challenges for the operations team.

Scenario - 3

Dave, a department head, identified a concern from the situation section in his hub. He thought the issue to be because of Team A so he cascaded Team A to improve on certain parameters.

Team A improved on all the parameters suggested by Dave, but the issue still exists.

What is the common point in all the three scenarios?

There is no standard problem-solving methodology followed. Let's have a quick look at the issues:

Scenario - 1: Temporary fix treated as a solution, no proper solution approach taken

Scenario - 2: Relying on a specialist to solve the problem

Scenario - 3: No root cause analysis performed, trying to resolve the concern based on perception.

These are pretty common approaches across industries hence it's required that problem-solving methodology be followed to reap the maximum benefit of visual management.

Why it's necessary?

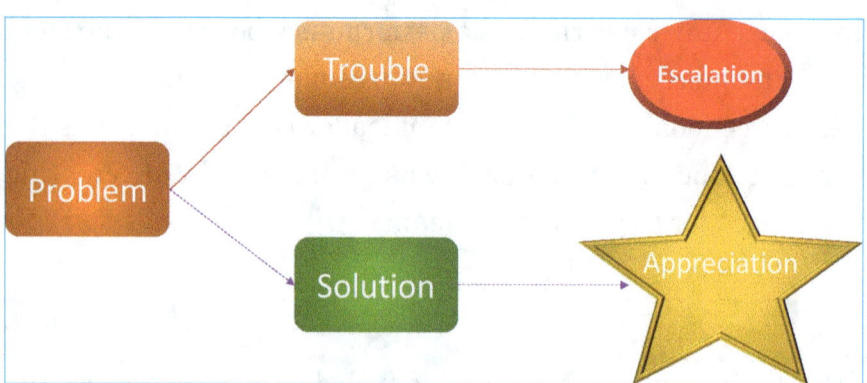

Which path will you choose?

Absolutely, the path to Appreciation...

Problem-Solving Vs FireFighting

❖ Problem-solving is a planned exercise to evaluate and understand a problem before countermeasures are introduced.

❖ Firefighting is a supportive exercise to maintain production with no adverse effects on quality.

Organizations with excellent visual boards and performance hubs could not reap the benefits of visual management because of lack of problem-solving approach from bottom to top.

How to make problem-solving a success?

1. Encourage team members to raise alarms – If your team is empowered enough that they can flag the concerns which are repetitive in nature and not accept them as BAU then be assured that you are marked green against one of the most critical success factors of problem-solving.

2. Incentivize the resources coming up with ideas and innovative thoughts – Root Cause analysis and solution identification are crucial for successful resolution of a problem. Hence it's important that you motivate your team members who propose new ideas and suggestions.

3. Shift from Specialist to Team Work – Never rely or give only a specific person the responsibility to resolve the problem. One person may have a limited horizon of thinking, but when a team works together you have a higher chance of getting a more robust solution. As the solution gets finalized, post lots of brainstorming and scrutiny, so the chances of fallback get reduced.

Now let's see the 5C approach of problem-solving which we have read in the previous chapter as well as under the Resolution section of the performance hub.

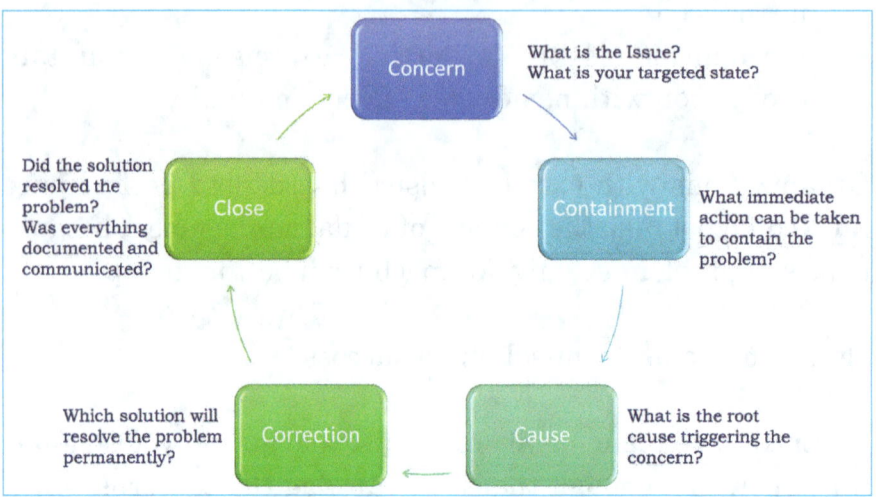

How to draft your concern?

It's said that 50% of your issue gets resolved if you can draft your problem statement properly.

Take Kipling's questions' help.

<u>What, why, when, how, where,</u> and <u>who</u>

- What is the problem?
- Why is it a problem?
- Where is it a problem?
- How is it a problem? (Quality, Cost, Delivery, Safety, Attrition, Morale, Motivation)
- When is it a problem?
- Who is it a problem for?

So, a sample problem statement and targeted state is as below:

<u>Problem Statement</u> – In the last 3 months, the number of escalations from the customer have gone up by 30%, from 20/month in Dec'17 to ~26/month average in Mar'18.

<u>Targeted State</u> – To reduce escalation level by ~50%, reducing it to below 15/month average by Jun'18.

Remember, the target you establish should be based on facts and not on your wish. The target set must be realistic, achievable and also a bit stretched which triggers lateral thinking.

You can also ascertain your last best performance before deciding the target.

What can be considered Containment here?

Probably to stop the customers from getting irate, you can appoint one additional resource in escalation handling for faster resolution of escalations till the time the issue is rectified.

Identify Cause:

Now that you have the problem statement and your targeted state, you need to perform analysis around high escalations.

CHAPTER 7

Collect data of the past three months of escalation and categorize them based on the reason of escalation.

Categories	Occurrence
Repeat Occurrence	27
Quality of resolution	22
Delayed resolution	15
Communication	5
Ticket closed without confirmation	4
High wait time on IVR	3
Confusing IVR	3

Since the above table is for illustration purpose only, the categories are few. Think about a scenario where you find more than 30 categories.

In that case, you need to collect the data and then plot a Pareto.

Vilfredo Pareto, an Italian economist, observed that 80% of the total Italian income was associated with only 20% of the population.

Thus, the 80:20 rule was born and can be used in many situations, which implies that approximately 80% of the total effect comes from about 20% of the possible causes.

For this analysis, you need to arrange the data in descending order and plot a Pareto Graph.

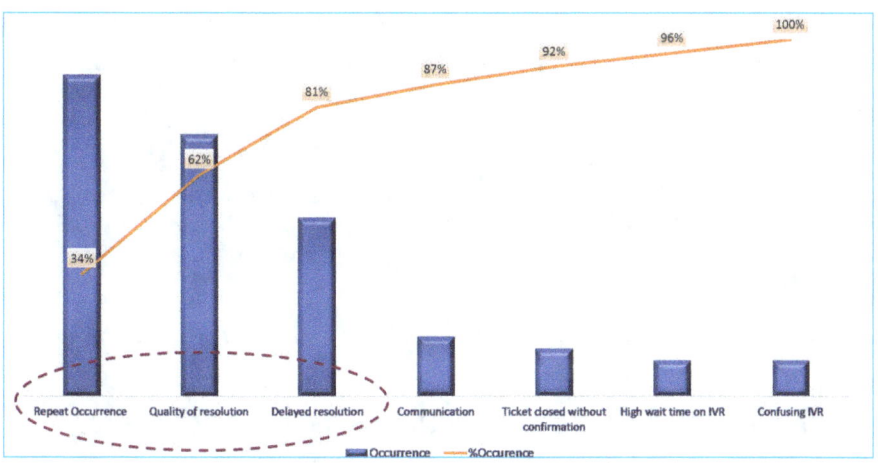

80% of the escalations are due to the following top three categories:

1. Repeat Occurrence
2. Quality of resolution
3. Delayed resolution

Now you have identified the three areas that are leading to escalations. Do you think this is the root cause?

No, you have to drill down further to understand why it's happening?

So what all tools one can use, to identify root cause once vital few are identified?

BRAINSTORMING

A technique where team members sit together and identify the root cause.

This technique helps in collecting all possible reasons associated to the problem, based on experience of the team members.

It can also be used while identifying the best possible solution to a problem whose root cause has been identified.

Image - https://humanresourcesblog.in/2016/07/24/the-art-of-brainstorming/

➢ **NEVER** criticize or judge the ideas of other people
➢ Get lots of ideas, however wild or crazy
➢ Record all ideas (on a board or flipchart)
➢ Build on the ideas of others

5 WHYS

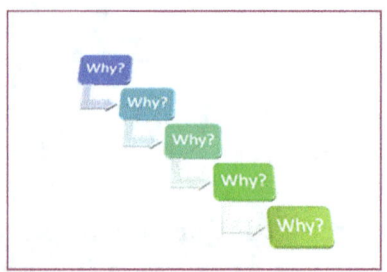

Gather data to determine the root cause.

To push for root causes, start with the problem you are trying to solve and then ask WHY (about) five times.

Whys can be increased to 6 and 7, what's important is that you ask the right why.

FISHBONE

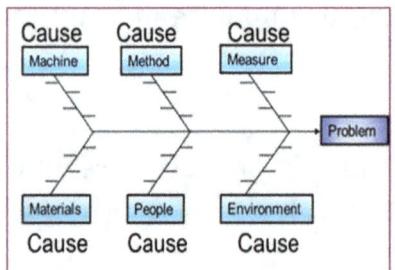

Also known as Ishikawa diagram or cause and effect diagram.

In this technique, you use data and brainstorming to identify causes. The cause can be related to either Machine, People, Materials, Method, Measure or Environment.

Categorise and display the possible causes.

Let's perform root cause analysis on the vital few that we have collated from the Pareto graph using fish bone.

So based on the vital few, you can invite your team members before the meeting to appraise them about the topic of discussion and expectation from them.

This will allow them to prepare themselves for the upcoming session.

You can start putting in the probable cause on this Fishbone.

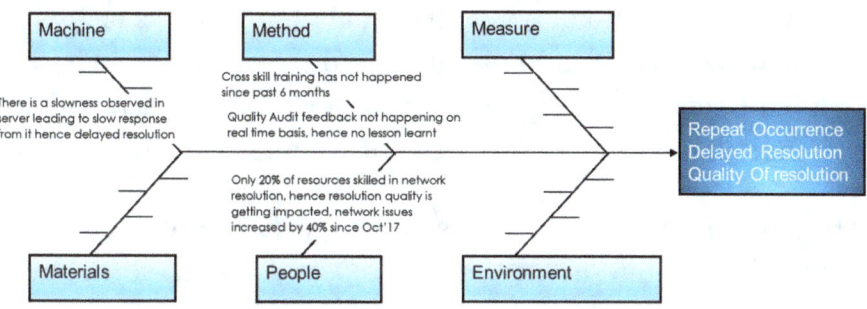

From the above Fishbone, you have identified four probable areas, to ensure that these are the areas leading to escalations. You can also use techniques like <u>Go & See.</u>

In this method, you need to be on the floor, take samples and validate the findings.

There are two such reasons where you can further drill down to understand the reason using the 5 whys before implementing any solution like:

1. Cross-skill training has not happened since the past six months – You need to ask the relevant owner 'Why has it not happened?' to understand the actual cause and implement a solution around it. You just cannot start cross-skill trainings one after another to address the issue, you

have to address the core reason, so that such kind of issues do not happen in future. And that can only happen once you have the answer to your question - why cross-skill training has not happened since the past six months?

2. Quality Audit feedback is not happening on real time basis, hence no lesson learnt – This is again a common scenario where managers start monitoring themselves to ensure that feedback is given on time. The process continues for few months and then everything falls back to status quo. It's important to understand why it's not happening. Is there any scope of automation so that real time feedback of quality audits can be given to resources and we can avoid such kind of misses going forward? Are there enough governance points in place to avoid such issues going forward?

The motive is to not stop at just the superficial layer, question them till you get the actual cause. Once you have the real cause only then your solution will be permanent, else you will always be in firefighting mode.

Correct

While identifying the solution, ensure that you are identifying the solution aiming it to be a permanent fix.

Prevention

➤ Make it impossible to make the error
➤ Make it harder to make the error

Detection

➤ Make it obvious that the error has occurred

No Impact

➤ Make the system robust so that it tolerates the error

Mistake Proofing Approach:

✓ Help people do the right thing by preventing them from doing the wrong thing (automation, physical restrictions, warnings, etc.)

✓ Create easy to follow and access standard work tools (Standard Operating Procedures, Checklists, Single Point Lessons)

✓ Provide adequate training and retraining (see, learn, do, teach, coach)

✓ Have customer requirement reviews/discussions with upstream suppliers

✓ Highlight problems, send work back upstream for completion and/or correction and follow up with additional training

Close

Once you implement the solution, observe for a certain timeframe. Based on the complexity and environment, you can decide your observation period, if there are behavioral changes then it generally takes time as compared to system changes or automation.

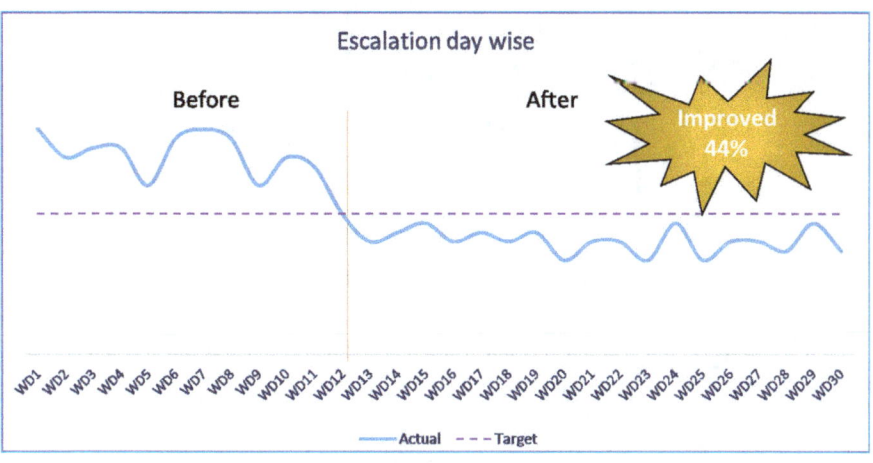

The key aspect for any problem that you want to resolve is, perform certain baselining, set a target around it, establish the root cause, identify a permanent solution, keep measuring the key metrics to ascertain whether the identified solution delivered the desired result or not.

Monitor it till the time you believe that the performance has become stable and is in control.

Close the problem with appropriate lessons learnt and share the best practices with the teams.

Celebrate the success and recognize the team members who played pivotal roles in resolving the problem.

KEY NOTES

- Define the problem.
- Measure the problem, perform baselining, identify the vital few.
- Set the targeted state.
- Establish the root cause, brainstorm potential causes.
- Narrow down the causal analysis, work through 5-Why to the root cause(s).
- Validate the identified root cause with Go & See.
- Correct – Identify the solution.
- Close – Validate the improvement and the benefits achieved.

QUIZ

1. **In 5C methodology which C comes first?**
   a. Concern
   b. Containment
   c. Cause
   d. Correct
   e. Close

2. **Containment is a permanent fix:**
   a. True
   b. False

3. **5C is completed post you apply the solution:**
   a. True
   b. False

4. **5C is a team leader's job:**
   a. True
   b. False

5. **Pareto chart is used during:**
   a. Concern
   b. Containment
   c. Both a & b
   d. None of the above

CHAPTER 7

6. **Ishikawa Diagram is also called:**
    a. 5 Whys
    b. Cause & Effect
    c. Fishbone
    d. Both b & c

7. **Men, Money, Material, Method, Environment are categories of:**
    a. 5 Whys
    b. Cause & Effect
    c. Go & See
    d. FMEA

8. **Brainstorming is only done during cause analysis:**
    a. True
    b. False

9. **Brainstorming is also a part of:**
    a. 5 Whys
    b. Fishbone
    c. Pareto
    d. Both a & b

WHY VISUAL MANAGEMENT FAILS

In the previous chapters we have seen, how to set up a visual board, run it and harness the benefits from it.

There are certain precautions which need to be taken to ensure that visual management does not fail.

As based on my experience and studying various blogs of eminent consultants, it's pretty evident that visual boards and the entire visual management process tend to fail after a certain period of time.

People at times either lose interest, or start customizing the entire process to suit their own convenience.

Let me share my experience with you about the failure reasons I have come across, followed by some more experiences from across the globe.

Common reasons of failure:

❖ Customizing the approach to suit own convenience: This situation can arise at any level of the organization, either the top management or at the bottom layer. I have seen managers changing the huddle timings of their own hub based on their convenience, and with time they start sending their subordinates in hub meetings. Performance Hub meetings demand strict adherence to schedule and timing. We all work in an environment where any critical issue can pop up at any time. Rescheduling it 2-3 times in a month is acceptable, but if you begin to reschedule your hub meeting daily, it shows that either you have not planned it properly or you are just conducting it for the sake of it.

❖ Metrics with No Target or Low Target – We already discussed in the earlier chapter that whatever metrics you put on visual boards, they must have targets associated to them. Some common excuses by Team Leaders and Managers have been encountered while setting targets around metrics:

- There are no targets given by the customer for this metric
- I am not aware of any target as my Operations lead has not given any target
- I cannot set any target as the team will feel burdened
- This target is too high to achieve

Regarding the first point that the customer has not given any target for this metric, this scenario is common as the targets agreed with customers are primarily on CTQs. To ensure that you meet the CTQs, you must measure the CTPs. Based on the CTQs' target, you have to decide the CTPs' target.

As mentioned in the earlier chapter, based on the objectives or customer's SLA, teams must have metrics associated with them, and these metrics are strongly correlated.

CHAPTER 8

For e.g. Your contract has 2 SLAs agreed with the customer

1. 95% of the tickets to be resolved within 4 hours
2. <5% Abandonment rate

To ensure that these metrics meet the targets, you will have several other CTPs which are correlated to it, like Productivity/resource, % Staff Availability, Unplanned Leaves, Demand Vs Capacity.

So it's the responsibility of the Operation Manager and the Team leader to set internal targets against these linked metrics, so that if they perform at the targeted level, you will meet the agreed SLA with the customer.

Let's elaborate about other scenarios, "*Cannot set any target as team will be burdened*" or "*This target is too high to achieve*".

Think about a scenario where someone comes to you and says that his team's Call Handling capacity/resource is 25/day.

What will you figure out from this? Is it good? Bad? You definitely need a figure to compare and comment on it.

Some leaders set very low targets, fearing that stretched targets may impact team morale. This quote really suits them.

"The greater danger for most of us lies not in setting our aim too high and falling short; but in setting our aim too low, and achieving our mark." - Michelangelo

CHAPTER 8

The reason visual board fails at times is when we set low targets and keep achieving them. This leads to no concern in complication and hubs become a boring area with no action, nor any problem-solving.

Remember, people don't lose interest because of any challenging work, they lose interest when the work becomes BAU with the same thing reflecting on boards.

Hence it's always recommended to review your targets and challenge the team to think in an innovative way, to achieve the targets. This will keep them busy in search of new ideas.

It's always good to ask the team to beat their own target and set a new one.

- ❖ Strict Mandate from the Management – At times the higher management pushes Visual management like a mandate and issues a notice to all the teams to have their boards updated. This generally leads to an eyewash exercise where boards are just updated to please the higher management.
- ❖ Contents of visual boards decided by a consultant – I have received such proposals where the Operations manager or the department head asked me to put all the content which I felt right to be on the board and provide it to them.

  Taking sessions on visual management, performance hub and engaging the team in various activities is the responsibility of the consultant. Post such sessions, designing the visual boards is the responsibility of the respective teams/departments/managers. The consultant facilitates the designing to ensure that proper lean approach is followed and is also a part of the performance hub for a certain time frame to provide feedback, so that the teams start following the right practices; it's more like hand-holding.

But if consultants start designing the entire boards, then the ownership factor will not be induced within the team members.

As we have discussed earlier, Visual Management is a philosophy, a cultural shift, and that requires acceptability. It's not a tool which can be downloaded at anybody's system.

Hence, it is ideal for the respective teams or users of visual boards to design their boards to create a sense of ownership and accountability.

* Visual Management is only for the Bottom Layer – This attitude is one of the key reasons for failure of visual management. I have mentioned in the previous chapters as well that Visual management must be implemented like a value chain flowing from the top to bottom and vice versa.

For a concern identified in the CEO's performance hub, the root cause can be from any layer of the organization. The correction to it will lead to action points for various departments. Similarly, the team at the bottom layer meeting its objectives has a ripple effect at the top.

Hence, it's utmost necessary that the top leadership also shows their commitments to visual management.

To be useful, the visual management approach must be based on a set of measurable objectives that the organization wants to achieve. It helps the organizations align the goals of every person and team with the strategic objectives of the organization as a whole. It also makes it easy to track the results of each improvement. What's more, it makes it easy for leaders to visualize the progress of improvement work itself. They get a view into the health of the organization and can readily identify, recognize and reward individuals who are making good things happen.

"Rushing to create a visual management system will result in visual clutter that does nothing to help workers or managers improve the way work is done. If you take your time establishing the right foundation, you'll be rewarded with visuals that help people do their jobs better."

Dan Markovitz, President of Markovitz Consulting, a faculty member at the Lean Enterprise Institute, and a teacher at the Stanford University

If the above mentioned areas are taken care of then definitely an organization will be in a situation to create an environment to run visual management effectively and efficiently.

KEY NOTES

- Visual Management should not be treated as a tool. It's an enabler, to improve performance at every layer.
- The cultural shift needs time, hence interest and ownership need to be induced.
- Create interesting and challenging visual boards.
- Top Management involvement is a must.

QUIZ

1. **Targets are not Mandatory for Metrics on Visual Boards:**
   a. Not Always Mandatory
   b. True
   c. Targets are Optional
   d. Always Mandatory

2. **Performance Hub meetings are done:**
   a. On as and when basis
   b. On Team Leader's availability
   c. During Customer Visit
   d. As per agreed frequency and slot

3. **Visual Management boards to be designed by Business Excellence Consultants for better results:**
   a. True
   b. False

4. **Performance Hub is not applicable for the CEO:**
   a. True
   b. False

5. **Targets on Performance Hubs:**
   a. To be revised at periodic intervals
   b. Should not be revised
   c. To be removed once the team start meeting targets
   d. Both a & c

CHAPTER 8

VISUAL BOARDS

In this chapter, we will go through some of the visual boards across industries. These are shared just for your reference as I pointed earlier that naming convention is not applicable for performance hubs. You can name your sections accordingly, but the important aspect is to follow the concept rightly.

Your performance hub should reflect three things:

1. Situation at a Glance
2. Expose Problems
3. Inspire for improvement

Let's see some visual boards/performance hubs.

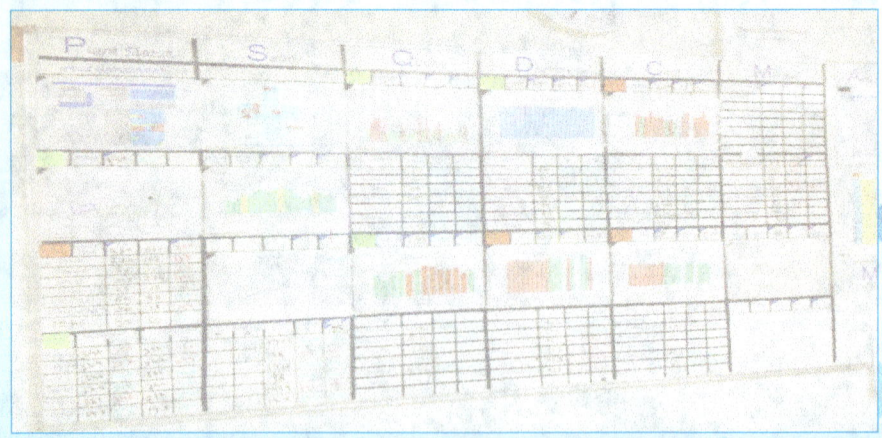

https://the-lmj.com/2013/07/hidden-in-plain-sight/3-psqdcm-board-fx-2013/

We can see:

- Appropriate usage of color to highlight issues if any.
- Hand written numbers, the daily measures and the trends to observe the pattern.

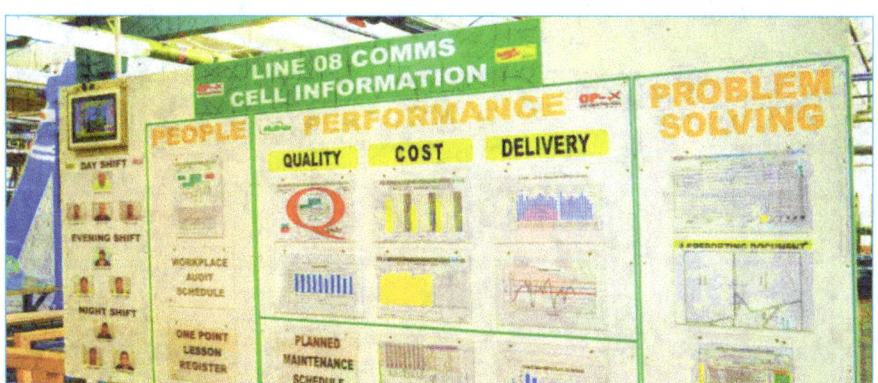

http://www.cmc-consultants.com/blog/lean-visual-management-boards-in-factories-keep-it-simple

Here the Situation section is named as Performance. Metrics are bucketed under three categories - Quality, Cost and Delivery.

Resolution section is termed as Problem Solving, to pull out any concerns from Performance to Problem Solving.

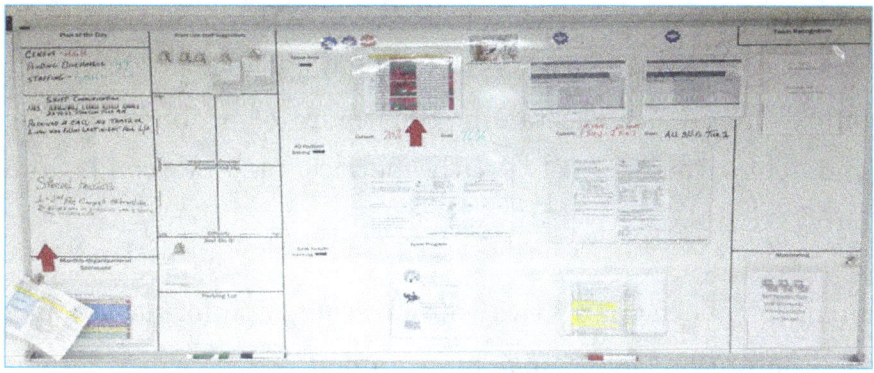

http://www.leanhealthcareexchange.com/wp-content/uploads/2015/03/LeanHealthcare_VisualManagement1RS.jpg

CHAPTER 9

Check the arrows on the board above showing current status and the goal.

There is also a section of Recognition, a must to boost your team morale.

https://www.industryforum.co.uk/resources/blog/10-ways-to-make-your-visual-management-boards-work/

This hub board also has metrics categorized under various sections.

There is a section called Improvement which holds all the improvement actions taken. It is more of problem solving and looks really lively, with metrics mix of trends and handwritten.

In all the above boards, way of representing information may be different but few things are common:

1. Liveliness of the boards

2. Boards have trends and color coding to ensure that if anything deviates from its required level, it can be noticed easily
3. Problem solving approach on these boards
4. Majority of the boards are on actual operation areas, and are not placed in a corner to ensure visibility
5. The cleanliness of the boards

QUIZ GUIDE

CHAPTER -1

Visual Management Is:

a. Nicely Painted Walls
b. Wall with Organization Objectives
c. Visual Boards (Electronic or Manual) with metrics and stuff to trigger proactive action if anything moves from its standard state
d. A notice board

Answer: C

Visual boards must follow the 3 ground rules:

- Situation at Glance
- Expose Problem
- Inspire Improvement

Visual Management not applicable in:

a. Manufacturing Industry
b. Automobile Industry

c. Healthcare

d. None of the above

Answer: D

Visual Management is applicable everywhere including your kitchen.

Visual Management is all about:

a. Bar charts and Pie charts on Boards

b. Putting Team Structure on a Board

c. Highlighting the Major Escalations

d. It's a combination of Team Objectives, Metrics, Issues and Key success

Answer: D

Visual Management is, where a team can relate to what they are doing and the purpose behind doing it, hence Objective is required. How we are performing on our objectives will be available in the Metrics section. What is stopping us from meeting our target will reflect in Issues section. And once the issues are resolved through problem-solving, it will lead to your success story.

Benefits of Visual Management:

a. Team Cohesiveness

b. Improves individual ownership and accountability

c. Focused and proactive approach

d. All of the above

Answer: D

Visual Management has multi-layered benefits, starting from mindset and behavior change to higher productivity.

Visual boards must be prepared with only Black and Blue Color:

a. True
b. False

Answer: B

Visual boards must be interesting and must have attractive look and feel.

Colors are also used to depict any positive or negatives, which serve the purpose of situation at a glance and expose problems.

CHAPTER -2

Visual boards are just for the team to view; action is to be taken only by leads in case of any deviation:

a. True
b. False

Answer: B

Visual boards are for the entire team; the ownership is of the team. It's not an individual's or specialist's work, it's team effort.

What information related to the team and customers can be displayed on visual boards:

a. All
b. Only the information which is relevant to the overall team and within the compliance guidelines
c. Individual information
d. None of the above

Answer: B

Putting all the information on a board will clutter it so only relevant information must be presented.

Information which is not allowed to be published on the floor must be published based on the compliance guidelines. Individuals' performance published to highlight the bottom performers should not be placed on boards.

For metrics on visual boards target or standards are not compulsory:

a. True
b. False

Answer: B

Without any target or standards, visual boards are just wallpaper. They neither trigger any action nor create any interest among the users.

The aim of visual boards is to showcase about the organization to potential customers during floor visits, which helps in gaining more business:

a. True
b. False

Answer: B

Aim of visual boards is to empower, motivate and encourage the respective teams to be the owners of excelling their own performance.

Aim of visual boards is to please the higher management:

a. True
b. False

Answer: B

QUIZ GUIDE

Aim of visual boards is to empower, motivate and encourage the respective teams to be the owners of excelling their own performance.

CHAPTER -3

System Thinking is only applicable in Healthcare:

a. True
b. False

Answer: B

System Thinking is the most critical thought process which enables right action at the right place at the right time.

System Thinking means understanding the interlinkage between various components and their impact on the end deliverable:

a. True
b. False

Answer: A

System Thinking is the most critical thought process which enables right action at the right place at the right time.

Displaying all possible metrics on board is the best example of System Thinking:

a. True
b. False

Answer: B

Displaying all the information on visual board only clutters the board.

Which approach must be taken to identify the metrics on visual boards based on the concept of system thinking:

a. Value chain mapping
b. Correlation Study
c. Ask the reporting manager
d. A & B

Answer: B

Interlinking between metrics and strong correlation among the metrics is important. Only then the improvement on one will have a ripple effect on others.

Every layer in the organization should measure similar metrics to maintain uniformity:

a. True
b. False

Answer: B

Every layer in the organization has a different objective, if all see the same metrics then it will not be meaningful and neither can they initiate any improvement at their level.

Visual Management based on system thinking helps in:

a. Driving Business Improvement from Bottom to Top and Vice Versa
b. Right action at the right place and the right time
c. Save time in identifying the root cause
d. All of the above

Answer: D

The improvement and the gains will form a value chain for the entire organization.

CHAPTER -4

The 1ˢᵗ step you take while implementing Visual Management:

a. Set objectives clear for the business
b. Set goals for individual departments
c. Create a plan for organization-wide implementation
d. Establish reasons for why Visual Management is necessary

Answer: A

It should start from the top, first objective for the business to be set up.

Why do you need goals for individual departments?

a. To please the higher management
b. To be audit compliant
c. To ensure department's focus on their goals and plan their governance plan accordingly
d. All of the above

Answer: C

Goals are for the department to work on, if they just work to please the higher management by showing wonderful presentations then with time the department will fail to perform and remain competitive.

Why is it recommended to implement visual management using the top down approach?

a. Visual management is a practice which requires commitment hence leaders need to lead by example
b. Deviation of metrics from the target at top will lead to cascading of right concerns to the right department for action

c. Higher management is more skilled

d. A & B

Answer: D

Skill is the secondary requirement for effective visual management, primary is the mindset for continuous improvement, openness and commitment.

Why is it necessary to establish the reason "Why Visual Management is necessary"?

a. For CMMI certification

b. To convince and engage the people across organization to be more participative, and harness the benefits of it

c. A & B

d. Only B

Answer: D

Participation of people across the organization is key to effective visual management.

Why is it necessary to engage team members in interactive session before implementing Visual management?

a. For better understanding of its objective

b. For encouraging more participation and inducing interest

c. To make them aware how visual management work

d. To make them understand it's not forced on them

e. All of the above

Answer: E

Participation of people and understanding of visual management across the organization are key to effective visual management.

CHAPTER -5

Why Objective Mapping necessary for individual teams with that of organization:

a. To form a complete value chain
b. So that appraisal hikes can be decided
c. To ensure that entire organization is working towards meeting the Organizations objective
d. To ensure team feels more accountable of their work
e. A, B, C, D
f. A, C, D

Answer: F

Linking items to appraisal hikes may not lead to continuous gain as for some people x% is a good hike, for some y%. Objective mapping is more important to bring ownership, accountability and sense of pride about the job an individual is doing.

CTQs can only be provided by the customer:

a. True
b. False

Answer: B

CTQs are not always provided by the customer. At times customers provide high level requirements, translating them in to measurable metrics is done by the organization.

Ensuring CTQs are meeting the target is more important than the associated CTPs:

a. True
b. False

Answer: B

CTQs and CTPs both are important. If you are not performing well on CTPs your CTQs will get impacted.

CTQs and CTPs are a classic example of:

a. System Thinking
b. Value Addition
c. Waste in process
d. All of the above

Answer: A

There are many CTPs which when work on the targeted state lead to successful linked CTQs. Hence to identify the correct CTP for a given CTQ is system thinking.

Correlation value of -0.7 between 2 metrics means:

a. Metrics are not correlated
b. Metrics are directly proportional to each other
c. Metrics are inversely proportion to each other
d. Strong Positive relationship

Answer: C

Negative correlation value means two variables are inversely proportional to each other.

Correlation value of 0.7 between 2 metrics means:

a. Metrics are not correlated
b. Metrics are directly proportional to each other
c. Metrics are inversely proportion to each other
d. Strong negative relationship

Answer: B

Positive correlation value means two variables are directly proportional to each other.

Correlation value of 0.02 between 2 metrics means:

a. Metrics are not correlated
b. Strong Positive relationship
c. Strong negative relationship
d. None of the above

Answer: A

To establish that the metrics are correlated you need to have a correlation value closer to +-1.

CHAPTER -6

Performance hubs can only be

a. Electronic
b. Physical Boards
c. Both Physical and Electronic
d. Either a or b

Answer: D

Based on the convenience, floor space availability and team location it can be physical or electronic.

Metrics in Situation section need to be derived from:

a. Complication
b. Objectives
c. Based on Manager recommendation
d. Both a & c

Answer: B

Objectives to be translated into metrics

Department head should not attend Operations Level Performance hub

a. True
b. False

Answer: B

Department head should attend operation level performance hub, not necessarily daily, but periodic visit a must.

Department heads performance hub to have all the metrics measured across all the teams within the department

a. True
b. False

Answer: B

Department head's performance hub should have metrics linked to the department's objective.

For a team hub within a department, objective section must have objectives linked to:

a. Organization's Objective
b. Department's Objective
c. Both a and b
d. Team leader's objective

Answer: B

The team's objectives must be linked with department's objectives and the department's objectives to be linked with the organization's goals.

For a department's hub within an organization objective section must have objectives linked to:

a. Organization's Objective
b. Department's Objective
c. Both a and b
d. Department's head objective

Answer: A

The team's objectives must be linked with department's objectives and the department's objectives to be linked with the organization's goals.

Situation Section must have the following:

a. Metrics linked to the Objective
b. Daily/Weekly and Monthly Trends of Identified metrics
c. Targets/Standards for every metric
d. All of the above

Answer: D

Refer chapter, Situation Section

Situation Section must have the top concerns:

a. True
b. False

Answer: B

Concerns are to be in the complication section.

Complication Section derives its input from:

a. Objective
b. Situation
c. Resolution
d. None of the above

Answer: B

Any metrics deviating from the targeted state will lead to concern.

If there are no concerns in the complication section yet the customer is unhappy that shows:

a. Metrics are not correctly aligned to the customer need/ objectives

b. Targets are too low for respective metrics
c. Measurement system is not correct
d. All of the above

Answer: D

All 3 possibilities can be there.

A concern which is not getting pulled out from situation section cannot be a part of Complication section:

a. True
b. False

Answer: B

It may happen that a situation has popped up due to any sudden change or environmental issues. The concern arising out of such things which impact the specific hub users can be a part of the complication section.

Resolution section is derived from:

a. Recognition
b. Situation
c. Complication
d. Objective

Answer: C

Concern triggers resolution.

Resolution section is not mandatory for performance hub

a. True
b. False

Answer: C

In the absence of resolution, people do not practice problem-solving but act as mere spectator of the metrics.

Recognition section is not mandatory for performance hub

a. True
b. False

Answer: B

Team recognition and celebrating success are mandatory to keep the engine of continuous improvement running.

Recognition section is derived from

a. Resolution
b. Situation
c. Complication
d. Objective

Answer: A

Team recognition and celebrating success are mandatory to keep the engine of continuous improvement running.

A performance hub must only use the following naming convention "Objective", "Situation", "Complication" and "Resolution"

a. True
b. False

Answer: B

Naming convention is not important in visual management. Teams across the globe use their own naming conventions, what's important is the concept and methodology.

Section which boost healthy team competition and morale of team members

a. Resolution
b. Situation

c. Recognition
d. Objective

Answer: C

Team recognition and celebrating success are mandatory to keep the engine of continuous improvement running.

CHAPTER -7

In 5C methodology which C comes first?

a. Concern
b. Containment
c. Cause
d. Correct
e. Close

Answer: A

Problem solving starts with a problem statement.

Containment is the permanent fix

a. True
b. False

Answer: B

Containment is a temporary workaround to arrest the problem till permanent resolution identified. It's like to stop the bleeding, till the patient reaches the clinic, to avoid further damage.

5C completed post you apply the solution

a. True
b. False

Answer: B

Once you apply a solution, you have to monitor to validate whether the targeted state, which you expect post the solution, is achieved or not. Till then 5C cannot be closed.

5C is a team leader's job;

a. True
b. False

Answer: B

Problem solving is a team job not that of any specialist.

Pareto chart is used during

a. Concern
b. Containment
c. Both a & b
d. None of the above

Answer: A

While defining the problem statement you need to identify the vital few, based on which you frame your problem statement and set targeted state post resolution.

Ishikawa Diagram is also called

a. 5 Why
b. Cause & Effect
c. Fishbone
d. Both b & c

Answer: D

Men, Money, Material, Method, Environment are categories of:

a. 5 Why
b. Cause & Effect

c. Go & See

d. FMEA

Answer: B

Cause & Effect/Fishbone diagram

Brainstorming is only done during cause analysis:

a. True

b. False

Answer: B

Brainstorming can also be done while finalizing the problem statement and identifying the solution.

Brainstorming is also a part of:

a. 5 Why

b. Fishbone

c. Pareto

d. Both a & b

Answer: D

5 Whys and fishbone both require brainstorming.

CHAPTER -8

Targets are not Mandatory for Metrics on Visual Boards

a. Not Always Mandatory

b. True

c. Targets are Optional

d. Always Mandatory

Answer: D

Without targets it's just a board triggering no action.

Performance Hub meetings are done:

a. As and when Basis
b. On Team Leader's availability
c. During Customer Visit
d. As per agreed frequency and slot

Answer: D

There must be commitment towards hub meetings.

Visual Management boards to be designed by Business Excellence Consultant for better results

a. True
b. False

Answer: B

Visual boards are the property of the respective teams. Consultant's role is to train and mentor the team on the concepts, not to design and run the boards.

Performance Hub not applicable for CEO

a. True
b. False

Answer: B

Performance Hub is applicable from top to bottom at every layer for the overall visual management effectiveness.

Targets On Performance Hubs:

a. To be revised at periodic interval
b. Should not be revised
c. To be removed once team start meeting targets
d. Both a & c

Answer: A

If the team meets all the targets, then choose revised targets based on the best repeatable. This not only gives new energy and challenge but creates an environment to think differently to meet new targets and goals.

FOR FURTHER READING:

Books:

- *OEM Principles of Lean Thinking - by George Trachilis*
- *Developing Lean Leaders at All Levels - by Jeffrey K. Liker and George Trachilis*
- *Performance Hubs: Engaging Teams in Focused Continuous Improvement – by Marc Roberts*

URLs:

- https://www.lean.org/shook/DisplayObject.cfm?o=2095
- https://blog.kainexus.com/continuous-improvement-software/visual-management/is-your-visual-management-board-doomed-to-fail
- http://gamep.org/wp-content/uploads/2015/01/Visual-Managment-Systems-Presentation.pdf

QUIZ GUIDE

www.ingramcontent.com/pod-product-compliance
Lightning Source LLC
Chambersburg PA
CBHW052327220526
45472CB00001B/302